Whispers of a Silent Monk

Poetic Tales of Love, Loss, and Liberation

SERIES I

Stories that speak in silence, poems that heal in stillness.

SHREE SHAMBAV

Whispers of a Silent Monk
Poetic Tales of Love, Loss, and Liberation Series I
Shree Shambav

Published by Shree Shambav, Tamil Nadu, India
Shree Shambav Ink & Imagination "Where Words Breathe and Imagination Soars"

First Edition, 2025

ISBN: 978-93-5619-425-0

Email:shreeshambav@gmail.com
Web:www.shambav.org

DEDICATION

"Isavasyam idam sarvam yat kim ca jagatyam jagat, tena tyaktena bhunjitha, ma gridhah kasyasvid dhanam"

To the Almighty,

the Divine Masters,

the family who listens,

and my parents who see –

your presence shapes the pages of my life's journey.

"Isavasyam idam sarvam yat kim ca jagatyam jagat"

Meaning: "God encompasses everything you perceive, see, or touch with your sense organs."

DISCLAIMER

This book was born from one such silence—not the silence of emptiness or isolation, but the silence that arrives when the noise of the world recedes, and the soul begins to listen. *Whispers of a Silent Monk* is not a manual, nor a doctrine. It is a gentle offering—a mirror to your own inner truth, a poetic invitation to return to the stillness within.

The character of the monk, Sahasrananda, is not to be idolised or followed. He is a reflection—his silence, a doorway to your own inner voice. Through parables, poems, and quiet reflections, this book hopes to stir what is already waiting within you: the wonder of the child, the longing of the seeker, and the wisdom of the soul.

The author and publisher expressly disclaim any liability for outcomes—personal, emotional, legal, spiritual, or otherwise—that may result from the interpretation or use of the ideas presented herein. These pages are not meant to replace professional advice in any field, including medical, psychological, legal, or financial.

Engaging with this book is an act of personal reflection. Its value lies not in prescribing answers, but in prompting deeper questions. It offers perspectives—some may resonate, others may not. Trust your discernment. Embrace only what aligns with your journey and release what doesn't.

We are honoured to share this space with you. May these words be a companion, not a compass—a quiet light guiding you back to the hidden sanctuary that has always been yours.

Note - If any part of the book, in any sequence, hurts the reader's sentiments, it would be just out of a sheer accident not intentional

EPIGRAM

In a world echoing with noise, the silent monk speaks through stillness, and his words arrive wrapped in poems, parables, and presence. His silence becomes a mirror, reflecting the love we forget, the pain we hide, and the freedom we seek. These whispers are not just stories—they are awakenings. For those who dare to listen, they offer not answers, but a return to what was never lost: the truth within.

– Shree Shambav

Whispers of a Silent Monk

Poetic Tales of Love, Loss, and Liberation

Shree Shambav

Shree Shambav is a 106x best-selling author renowned for his transformative works in personal development and spiritual growth.

Dear Cherished Readers

Dear Cherished Readers,

As I embark on this new literary voyage, my heart swells with profound gratitude and an overwhelming sense of connection. With deep emotion, I extend my heartfelt appreciation to each of you who has joined me on this journey.

With sincere warmth, I invite you to revisit the steps we have taken together through the pages of my earlier works. Our odyssey began with "Journey of Soul - Karma," a book that marked my first foray into the world of words and a testament to the raw passion that ignited my writing adventure.

The subsequent chapters of our shared journey unfolded through the enchanting tapestry of the *"Twenty + One"* series. With each page turned, it felt as though a brushstroke was added to the canvas of our collective imagination—stories and sentiments woven to echo within the quiet corners of your heart. These weren't just words; they were invitations to feel, to reflect, and to remember what truly matters.

And how can I not cherish the transformative path we walked together through the *"Life Changing Journey—Inspirational Quotes Series?"* Day by day, quote by quote, we ventured inward—into spaces often overlooked—to find wisdom in simplicity and light in life's shadows. Each reflection was offered as a gentle whisper of hope, a spark meant to uplift, inspire, and remind us that even in silence, the soul speaks.

The release of "Death - Light of Life and the Shadow of Death" promises to shed new light on the timeless mystery of death.

The **Optimum Python Series** is a comprehensive guide designed to empower readers at every stage of their programming journey. It begins with *Series I: Ultimate Guide for Beginners*, which lays a strong foundation in Python, making it accessible and engaging for newcomers. *Series II: Exploring Data Structures and Algorithms* takes the next step, offering a deep dive into core computer science principles that enhance problem-solving skills and coding efficiency. Building on this, *Series III: Python Power for Data Science* introduces powerful libraries such as NumPy, Pandas, Matplotlib, and Scikit-learn, guiding readers through data manipulation, visualisation, and foundational machine learning techniques. Finally, *Series IV: Unleashing the Potential of Data Science with Machine Learning Techniques* explores advanced machine learning models and real-world applications, enabling readers to harness the full potential of data-driven insights. Whether you're just starting out or looking to master sophisticated tools and strategies, this series is your roadmap to Python proficiency and beyond.

Shree Shambav expands his artistic repertoire with *Whispers of Eternity: A Symphony of Soulful Verses*, a heartfelt exploration of the human experience expressed through lyrical depth and timeless reflection. Complementing this, his *Whispers of the Soul: A Journey Through Haiku* distils profound truths into delicate, poignant verses, capturing the fleeting essence of life with elegant simplicity.

Equally evocative, *Whispers of Stillness: Where the Soul Listens Beyond the Noise* offers meditative couplets that invite readers into silence, where wisdom blossoms in the spaces between words. Together, these works illuminate Shambav's versatility and mastery of soulful expression. They invite readers on a transformative journey of self-discovery, weaving a tapestry of emotion, insight, and transcendence that lingers long after the final page is turned.

Building on this success, he continued to enchant audiences with his subsequent albums: HeartStrings, *Melodies of the Heart*, *Driftwood Memories*, *Winds of Change*, *The Veil and the Waves*, *Echoes of the Soul*, *Phoenix Within*, Uncaged, Where Nature Sings and Wings of Forever. Each album further solidified his place in the world of music, offering a mesmerising collection of tracks that evoke nostalgia, introspection, and heartfelt connection. With every composition, Shree Shambav weaves a musical journey that lingers in the soul long after the final note fades.

Shree Shambav's latest works shine as luminous beacons on the path of self-discovery, mindful living, and spiritual awakening. His writings span a vast spectrum of human experience, each book offering a doorway to transformation. Among his most celebrated titles are Learn to Love Yourself: A Journey of Discovering Inner Beauty and Strength Through 10 Transformative Rules, The Power of Letting Go: Embrace Freedom and Happiness, A Journey of Lasting Peace, and The Entitlement Trap: Get Over It, Get On.

His thought-provoking works include Whispers of a Dying Soul: Unspoken Regrets and Unlived Dreams, Whispers of Silence: Unlocking Inner Power through Stillness, The Power of Words: Transforming Speech, Transforming Lives, The Art of Intentional Living: Minimalism for a Life of Purpose, and Awakening the Infinite: The Power of Consciousness in Transforming Life.

In The Power of Manifestation: Unlocking the Path from Thought to Reality, Shree Shambav offers a transformative roadmap for turning vision into reality, while Beyond the Veil: A Journey Through Life After

Death explores the profound mystery of what lies beyond earthly existence. His other powerful works include Bonds Beyond Blood: Where Love Builds Bridges and Bonds Defy Blood, a celebration of love that transcends lineage, The Inner Battlefield: Overcoming the Enemies of the Mind and Soul, a guide to conquering inner conflicts, and A Journey into Spiritual Maturity: 12 Golden Rules for Inner Transformation, which offers timeless wisdom for the evolving seeker. In The Seeker's Gold: Unlocking Life's Greatest Treasure, he inspires readers to discover the hidden riches of the soul, while The Law of Attraction: A Soulful Path reveals how to harmonise thought, energy, and intention to create a life aligned with one's highest purpose. His transformative Born to Rise series further empowers readers to embrace growth, clarity, and lasting fulfilment.

In addition to these works, Shree Shambav has recently ventured into astrology with the release of Astrology Unveiled – Foundations of Ancient Wisdom Series I to XIX, expanding into the realm of metaphysics. These books explore the foundational principles of Vedic astrology, offering readers a rich and practical understanding of this ancient wisdom.

Your unwavering support, enthusiasm to immerse yourself in my writings, and readiness to embark on these journeys with me have been my greatest sources of inspiration. Your input has been a beacon guiding me through the creation process, moulding these stories into containers of passion, emotion, knowledge, and resonance.

As I unveil this new narrative before you, know that your presence, insights, and shared moments have been my companions. The path we have walked together is etched in the annals of my creative evolution, and it's an honour beyond words to have you by my side once more.

Here's to the readers who have illuminated my path with their presence, who have embraced my stories with open hearts, and who have woven themselves into the very fabric of my literary world. Our journey has been a symbiotic dance of writer and reader, a harmony of souls brought together by the magic of storytelling.

With a heart brimming with appreciation and eyes glistening with anticipation, I extend my deepest gratitude for your unwavering support. Thank you for the memories, the shared emotions, and the countless hours spent in the worlds we've crafted together. As we step into this new adventure, let's continue to explore, feel, and discover the boundless horizons that words can unveil.

Warmly,

Shree Shambav

Suggested Reads

FROM BEST-SELLING AUTHOR

Endorsements

Whispers of a Silent Monk is a luminous blend of poetry, parable, and spiritual reflection. With rare grace and emotional depth, Shree Shambav invites us into a village transformed by silence, compassion, and timeless wisdom. Each chapter is a meditative journey into the heart's questions—of love, loss, identity, and liberation. This book doesn't just speak to the soul; it listens with it. A masterwork of gentle storytelling and profound insight, it reminds us that sometimes, the most powerful truths are whispered—not shouted. A must-read for seekers, dreamers, and those yearning for a deeper, quieter way of being.

— Lalitha

PREFACE

This book began, not with a plan, but with a stillness.

For years, I carried questions within me—unanswered, restless, raw. Not questions of the intellect, but of the soul. Why do we hurt? Why do we love with such intensity, only to lose? Is silence absence—or the most sacred presence? In seeking answers, I stumbled not upon doctrines, but upon stories. And among those stories, a figure emerged—not larger than life, but deeper than it. A monk with no name at first, no scriptures, no disciples. Only a presence. And soon, he was whispering through every page.

He came to be known as *Sahasrananda*—not because he called himself so, but because others did. A monk of a thousand joys, a thousand silences. He wandered not to teach, but to listen. He spoke not to impress, but to illuminate. Children loved him. The broken found solace beside him. The powerful, unsettled by him. But he judged no one. His wisdom came not from books, but from rivers, trees, laughter, and loss. And it is his journey—his gentle, unassuming, inward revolution—that fills these pages.

This book is the first in a series. Each volume stands as a doorway into a different phase of spiritual unfolding. *The Monk Who Planted Silence*, the first, lays the roots—it is about the beginning: of questioning, of wonder, of returning to the essence that the world makes us forget.

Structured into three parts—**Roots of Inner Awakening**, **Blooms of the Heart**, and **The House the Soul Built**—this work merges parables, poems, and philosophical reflections to touch the emotional, the spiritual, and the human. You'll meet villagers, seekers, lovers, kings, and children—each drawn into the orbit of this silent monk, each changed in ways they cannot always name.

But this is not just his story.

This book invites *you*—the reader—to walk beside him. To feel his silences like mirrors. To wrestle with your own questions through his simplicity. The stories are neither sermons nor solutions. They are invitations—to remember what you have forgotten, to grieve what you've buried, to dance where you once stood still.

You may find that the monk doesn't teach in traditional ways. He may answer a question with a story, respond to sorrow with a flower, or say nothing at all. But you will feel seen. You will feel heard. And in that space between his stillness and your breath, something may shift.

This book is a blend of fiction and spiritual reality. Though the monk never lived in the way we define "real," his presence is alive in each one of us who seeks truth with gentleness. In that sense, Sahasrananda is not a character. He is a possibility. A remembering. A return.

If you are holding this book, something within you is ready. Not to be taught, but to be reminded. Not to be led, but to be reawakened.

May these tales be a companion to your inner journey—through forests of doubt, deserts of grief, gardens of love, and the wide, open sky of silence.

With gratitude and encouragement,

Shree Shambav

INTRODUCTION

There are voices in the world that shout—and then, there are those that whisper. This book is born from the latter. *Whispers of a Silent Monk* is not a tale in the ordinary sense. It is a gathering of wind, of wisdom, of the sacred silences between questions and answers. It is the fragrance of a monk who never preached, yet transformed a kingdom—one still step, one silent glance, one loving word at a time.

This is the first in a series of poetic journeys centred around **Sahasrananda**, a wandering monk who settles in a quiet village nestled beneath the shade of ancient trees and beside the flow of a timeless river. His presence is simple, his speech sparse. Yet those who sit with him feel stirred, challenged, and often changed—not by persuasion, but by something deeper: a remembering of their own forgotten truths.

Part One: Roots of Inner Awakening traces the beginning of this transformative presence. It does not begin with grand miracles or thunderous revelations, but with gentle stirrings. The questions we so often silence—*Who am I? Why do I suffer? What is peace?*—are welcomed here like returning birds. Through stories of planting trees, listening to elders, flowing with life, and entering stillness, this part invites the reader into the sacred soil where the seed of awakening lies dormant, waiting for rain.

Part Two: Blooms of the Heart delves into the intimate terrain of love and longing. Here, the monk speaks not in doctrines, but in parables and poetry that bloom from the heart's deepest ache. We witness love in its divine fullness—as crucifix and crown, as journey and surrender. From the tender awe of marriage to the eternal flame of a child's wonder, each chapter reflects how love, when unguarded, becomes a spiritual path.

Part Three: The House the Soul Built is a return inward. The stories and poems here explore the meaning of home—not just as a place of walls and roofs, but as a sanctuary of memory, longing, and return. These chapters are woven with metaphors of meadows, fire, thread, and ocean tides. They reflect on legacy, impermanence, and the quiet majesty of a life lived in presence. It is in this section that the silent monk becomes not only a teacher, but a mirror—a symbol of what remains when all else fades.

Throughout this book, each chapter pairs a soulful tale with a poem that echoes its heart. The stories are not linear; they flow like rivers—intersecting lives, questions, and realisations. Each poem is a pause, an inhalation, a chance to listen more deeply. And through them all runs a quiet current—the belief that in silence, there is truth, and in truth, there is liberation.

This book is for seekers. For those tired of noise. For those who carry unanswered questions like lanterns through nights. For those who've known love, loss, joy, and grief—not as obstacles, but as doorways. It is for the ones who have sat beside rivers and felt they were being spoken to.

In these whispered pages, may you find echoes of your own voice. And perhaps, in the stillness between words, the beginning of your own silent song.

Welcome home.

With warmth and sincerity,

Shree Shambav

PROLOGUE

The Arrival of Silence

No trumpet announced his coming. No banner carried his name. He walked barefoot, wrapped in white robes faded by time, his presence quieter than a falling leaf. The villagers first saw him at dawn—standing by the river, hands folded in prayer, not to a god, but to the silence itself.

They called him *Sahasrananda*, though he never uttered it himself. The name came from the elder who once dreamt of a monk with a thousand joys hidden in his still eyes.

He spoke not in words, but in gestures. He taught not with doctrine, but with living example. When children asked questions, he responded with a story. When elders wept, he simply sat beside them until their grief, too, fell quiet. The birds seemed to follow him. The trees leaned slightly where he walked.

One morning, he planted a seed at the edge of the village—a single act, done without ceremony. No one asked what it was. But over time, that patch of earth grew into a garden. And around that garden gathered hearts in search of healing, minds in search of meaning.

Stories began to form. Not of miracles, but of moments—small, sacred, and deeply human. A widow found peace in a poem. A child asked about God and learned about stillness. A couple rediscovered each other through silence. These moments, like the petals of a lotus, slowly unfolded.

This book is the fragrance of those petals. These are the whispers of a silent monk.

CONTENTS

DEDICATION iii

DISCLAIMER v

EPIGRAM vii

Dear Cherished Readers xi

Suggested Reads xvii

Endorsements xix

PREFACE xxi

INTRODUCTION xxv

PROLOGUE xxix

CONTENTS xxxi

The Monk Who Planted Silence 1

PART ONE 5

- Roots of Inner Awakening 5

CHAPTER I 7

- Who Am I? 7

CHAPTER II 17

- The Wisdom of Elders 17

CHAPTER III 27

- He Who Plants a Tree 27

CHAPTER IV 37

Why Meditation? 37

CHAPTER V 51

Embracing Life's Flow 51

CHAPTER VI 61

The Eternal Stillness 61

PART TWO 69

BLOOMS OF THE HEART 69

CHAPTER VII 71

Love: Crown and Crucifix 71

CHAPTER VIII 85

A True Love's Odyssey 85

CHAPTER IX 97

Marriage: A Temple of Two Pillars 97

CHAPTER X 111

The Child Within 111

CHAPTER XI 129

Live Like a Flower 129

CHAPTER XII 141

Ashes and the Lamp 141

PART THREE 153

The House the Soul Built 153

CHAPTER XIII 155

Home: More Than Shelter 155

CHAPTER XIV 169

Roots and Wings 169

CHAPTER XV 187

The Threads We Leave Behind 187

CHAPTER XVI 199

The Sea Within Us 199

CHAPTER XVII 213

The Meadow Within 213

CHAPTER XVIII 231

The Fire That Fades 231

CHAPTER XIX 249

The Throne and the Puddle 249

Author's Note 253

Life Coach and Philanthropist 255

ACKNOWLEDGEMENTS 259

The Monk Who Planted Silence

"He planted more than trees—he planted silence, patience, and presence. And from those seeds, peace bloomed."

- Shree Shambav

Once, in a time long forgotten by most, a solitary monk named **Sahasrananda**—a wanderer not of maps, but of the soul—arrived at the borders of the **Kingdom of Aaditya**. The land was nestled between towering mountains, their snow-kissed peaks standing like silent sentinels of time. The kingdom, under King Aaditya, was a realm of harmony—its people content, its granaries full, its hearts light. But even in a land of plenty, not all questions are answered by abundance.

Sahasrananda found himself drawn to a secluded clearing just beyond a humble village, where the mountains whispered secrets only silence could hear. With no announcement and no ambition, he chose a spot beneath an ancient banyan tree and began to settle—not with noise, but with presence.

Each morning, long before the sun had stirred the sky, he would awaken during **Brahma Muhurta**, that sacred hour when the veil between the worlds is thinnest. There, under the sprawling arms of the banyan, he would sit—not to escape the world, but to listen more deeply to it. The wind, the leaves, the distant cries of birds—all became hymns in his vast inner temple.

During the day, he built himself a modest hut—not for shelter alone, but as a symbol of rootedness, a quiet sanctuary in a world always rushing. He planted saplings with the same care one might offer to a wounded child. Each seed, each handful of soil, was touched with reverence, as if he were helping the earth remember her own beauty.

People from the nearby village would sometimes pass him—some curious, some sceptical, some indifferent. To some, he was a mad wanderer who had renounced everything. To others, a holy man in disguise. But to most, he was simply "the silent one."

Yet, something in the space around his hut began to change. What was once dry and barren slowly transformed into an oasis of peace. Trees blossomed, birds made their home, and even the wind seemed to soften its voice there. The place no longer felt like a corner of the kingdom—it felt like a breathing presence, like the heart of the mountain itself had begun to beat there.

PART ONE

Roots of Inner Awakening

"Your identity is not what the world paints on your mirror—it is the clear gaze beneath the dust of time."

- *Shree Shambav*

CHAPTER I

Who Am I?

"The journey begins when the question 'Who am I?' is asked not from fear, but from wonder."

- *Shree Shambav*

The garden that once held only silence and wild earth had become a cradle of peace. What the monk built was not just a sanctuary of trees and flowers—it was a breathing hymn of stillness. The wind seemed to slow when it passed through the flowering plants. Birds sang as if the branches were sacred altars. Even the soil smelled different—like memory, like something ancient remembered.

Children, drawn by an unseen melody, began visiting the garden. Not for teachings, but for the butterflies that danced like painted dreams, and the dragonflies that skimmed across the air like tiny monks in flight. Laughter echoed through the air, delicate and free.

Some parents watched with concern, unsure of the quiet stranger. Others, sensing something beyond reason, allowed their children to go—perhaps believing, deep down, that this monk was not merely a man, but a mirror held by the universe.

One dusky evening, beneath the old banyan whose roots seemed to drink moonlight, Sahasrananda sat in still meditation. The breeze caressed the hem of his robe like a respectful disciple. Around him, the children played, their joy a soft halo. Among them was a curious child named **Aadhya**—bright-eyed, thoughtful, with a spark of yearning in her voice.

She approached the monk quietly, as if afraid to disturb the silence that felt like a living presence.

"**Guruji, who am I?**" she asked, her voice barely more than a whisper.

Sahasrananda opened his eyes slowly. They were not eyes that answered questions—they were eyes that had seen beyond them. He smiled, not with lips, but with presence.

He pointed toward a small mirror hanging near the doorway of his hut—old, weathered, forgotten.

"Let me tell you a story, Aadhya," he said. "Once, a mirror was placed in the corner of a room. Dust slowly gathered over it. Years passed. People walked by, forgetting it was ever a mirror. They saw the dust and assumed that was all it was—a dusty wall. But one day, someone wiped it clean… and for the first time, the mirror reflected light again. Their face. The sky. The truth."

He looked at her gently.

"You are that mirror. The dust is your name, your age, your school marks, your fears, and the praise people give you. None of it is you. Wipe it gently, every day, with silence. One day, you will see who you truly are."

A hush fell over the children.

The breeze whispered through the banyan leaves as Sahasrananda slowly opened his eyes. He did not answer in words alone—but in remembrance, as if reciting from the silence etched within his soul.

A young child turned with wonder wide to ask an old man still,

"Who are you, O silent sage, whom time has failed to still?"

The old man laughed—a tender sound, like wind through drifting sky,

"How can I name what I have shed, or name the reason why?"

I am not mind, nor fleeting thought, nor memory's fragile flame,

Not ego's pride, nor intellect, nor any changing name.

I am not sound, nor taste, nor sight, nor scent the wind may kiss—
Beyond all sense, beyond all form, I am eternal bliss.

I am not breath, nor vital force, nor form of flesh and bone,
Not bound by layers sheathed in skin, nor by the self I've known.
No limb or organ claims my soul, no weight my being bears,
For I am light, untouched by time, beyond both needs and cares.

No lust, no hate resides in me, no hunger or desire,
No pride to bind, no envy's flame, no ever-thirsting fire.
Not wealth, nor loss, nor worldly roles can tell you who I be—
I dwell beyond both gain and lack, in pure serenity.

Not sin nor virtue mark my path, nor sorrow, joy, or chain,
No need for chants or temple steps to wash away a stain.
I need no rite, no sacred text to teach me what is true—
For I am That which always was, and ever will be too.

No birth have I, no death to fear, no caste, nor name, nor creed,
No boundaries hold what I become, nor hunger, want, or need.
I am the all, yet not a thing—no shape, no line, no hue—

I am the stillness in the breath, the One in all of you.

The silence that followed was not empty—it was full, like the pause between heartbeats. Aadhya, along with other children, sat wide-eyed, the question no longer needed an answer. It had become a mirror.

Just then, an old man named Ramesh, who had been sitting at a distance—once sceptical, now softened—stepped forward.

"**Guruji, in what ways do we confuse the dust of roles, names, and experiences with our true self?**" he asked.

Sahasrananda turned toward him, his gaze kind and penetrating.

"We are like actors," he said, "who forget the stage is not the world. We wear roles—father, mother, king, beggar—and believe the costume is the soul. The dust settles slowly, each particle a story we think we are. But the soul is untouched. The dust cannot stain the sky."

He paused, placing his hand gently on his heart.

"To awaken is not to become something new, but to remember who you've always been."

As the golden hour settled gently on the earth, painting the garden in hues of fire and forgiveness, the wind quieted, as if the trees themselves leaned in to listen. The monk's story about the dusty mirror had not just touched Aadhya—it had stirred something in everyone present. Silence now hovered in the air, not as an absence of sound, but as a sacred presence.

An **elderly woman named Padma**, her silver hair braided with the grace of time, stepped forward slowly. Her eyes were weary, not just with age, but with years of searching—through roles played, sorrows endured, and joys that felt like borrowed light. She folded her hands and bowed gently.

"**Guruji,**" she said, her voice trembling like a candle in still air, **"How can silence and self-reflection become tools to uncover our unchanging inner essence?"**

The monk looked at her with great tenderness, as one might gaze at a river returning to its source after a long journey through lands and storms.

He gestured toward the **still pond** just beyond the banyan tree.

"Come, let us look together," he said.

They walked in quiet steps. The children followed. The sky had turned a dusky violet, and the pond mirrored it like a dream held in glass.

"Look into the water," he whispered.

She did.

"What do you see?"

"My reflection," she replied.

He picked up a small pebble and gently tossed it into the water. Ripples spread, blurring her image.

"Now?"

"It's distorted. I can't see clearly."

He nodded.

"This is the mind when filled with noise—thoughts, judgments, expectations, regrets. When we constantly speak or listen to the world outside, it's like throwing stones into the pond. The reflection—the self—disappears in the ripple."

She looked on, silently.

"But," he continued, "when we sit in **silence**, when we reflect without chasing every thought, the ripples settle. The water becomes still. And in that stillness, the **true face** appears—not the one made of age or memory, but the eternal one."

A soft gasp passed through the gathering, not out of surprise, but recognition—like a long-lost name remembered suddenly in a dream.

"Silence is not emptiness," he said. "It is the sky without clouds. It is not the absence of something, but the **presence of everything essential**."

His voice is now a hush merging with the wind.

"Self-reflection is the mirror. Silence is the light. Together, they reveal what has always been there, hidden beneath the noise—the soul, untouched by time, unburdened by name, free."

The old woman sat down, tears streaming down her cheeks—not of sorrow, but of homecoming.

And in that sacred moment, none spoke. The silence became the answer they all carried home within.

The days turned to weeks, and the quiet presence of the old monk, Sahasrananda, began to ripple through the nearby village like the fragrance of jasmine carried by the breeze—soft, invisible, yet unmistakably real.

What began as mere curiosity—a lone figure meditating beneath a banyan tree—soon deepened into quiet reverence. Ramesh, a thoughtful elder known for his integrity, who had once approached the monk with a question still echoing in his heart, would often pause near the garden to observe. He watched how the monk greeted even the smallest of beings—a caterpillar on a leaf, a thirsty sparrow—with the same reverence he had offered to a child's innocent query or a seeker's silent pain.

Padma, a gentle woman who had lived through storms of both joy and sorrow, had once come with her granddaughter, drawn by the stillness she could not name. After her question to the monk, something within her had softened—something long held and heavy. She now returned often, not to speak, but simply to sit in the hush that hung like incense beneath the banyan tree. Watching Sahasrananda water the plants with deliberate care, as if each leaf carried a hidden scripture, still brought tears to her eyes. "He is no ordinary wanderer," she had whispered once. "He is not less than a great sage."

Word spread—not as gossip, but as quiet awe. Like a spring uncovered after a long drought, people began arriving not with demands, but with silence. They came not to receive miracles but to sit in the presence of something long forgotten—the echo of stillness in a noisy world.

Some brought their burdens and left without speaking a word. Others brought their children, hoping they might learn something more enduring than what books and schools could offer. There were no sermons, no rituals, no proclamations of truth. Just the monk, seated in the shade of the ancient tree, his eyes half-closed, as if listening to a song only the soul could hear.

And something began to change—not in the monk, but in the people.

Conversations softened. Children played more gently. Neighbours began to greet each other with eyes that truly saw. The monk had not taught them what to do—but he had reminded them how to be. It was as though his silence became a mirror, quietly returning each soul to its original face.

Where there had once been a forgotten patch of land on the edge of the village, now bloomed a sanctuary—not built by hands, but by the slow and patient work of presence. Butterflies danced in the air. The wind carried the sound of distant bells. Even the sky seemed to bend closer, listening.

And every morning, as the stars faded, and the sun kissed the dew-soaked earth, Sahasrananda still sat beneath the banyan tree—like a mountain dressed in humility, like the ocean disguised as a cup of still water.

And slowly, the village remembered what they had forgotten—that wisdom does not shout; it whispers.

CHAPTER II

The Wisdom of Elders

"When roots run deep, the tree does not fear the wind. So too with the soul touched by ancient truths."

– Shree Shambav

Under the wide embrace of the ancient banyan tree—whose roots clutched the earth like memory holding time—Sahasrananda sat beside the village elders. His posture was simple, his eyes soft with listening. Around him, the garden echoed with the laughter of children, the fluttering wings of butterflies, and the low murmur of wind threading through leaves like forgotten songs.

But in that moment, the monk's attention was not on the rustling branches or the dancing light—it was on the gathering of elders who had begun to return to this sacred space, drawn like rivers to their original source.

They spoke not to impress, but to remember.

One elder, his hands rough with years of tilling the land, spoke of an herb once used to soothe a child's fever—a plant now nearly forgotten. Another recalled a ritual from his grandmother's time, where the full moon was honoured with song and silence. A woman with silver in her braid shared the names of rivers that no longer ran, yet still lived in her voice like lullabies.

And Sahasrananda listened—not with ears alone, but with his whole being. His stillness was not absence, but a sacred vessel. Like a mountain that hears the wind without moving, he received each word, each pause, each tear-laced smile, as if it were scripture.

The children, who usually raced past in bursts of restless energy, slowed their steps. Something about the way the monk sat, how the elders spoke, made them curious—not in mind, but in spirit. One child, dusty from play, sat cross-legged at a distance, glancing shyly. Another came closer, resting her head against her grandmother's knee. Slowly, they gathered like petals returning to the flower.

No one told them to be quiet.

But the hush came, not from instruction—but from reverence.

It was as if they knew, without knowing, that something sacred was happening—not in the form of lessons, but in the rhythm of remembrance. There were no blackboards or chalk, no doctrines or declarations—only stories woven from breath and time, and a monk who sat like the space between notes in a song.

In that shared silence, generations touched. Memory became medicine. Presence became prayer.

And the garden, once a simple patch of soil, became a sanctuary—a classroom of the soul, where the curriculum was carried in wrinkles, rooted in soil, and sung in silence.

Among them, Vasudevan, usually light-hearted and quick with questions, looked thoughtful. His gaze was fixed on the folds of his grandfather's worn shawl, on the lines etched into the faces of the village elders who sat nearby—lines carved not by time alone, but by love, by loss, by living fully.

He raised his hand gently and asked, "Guruji, in a world that chases what is new—new gadgets, new trends, new knowledge—how can we rediscover the sacredness of what is old and time-worn? How can we truly value the wisdom that is wrapped in age?"

There was a long pause.

Guruji closed his eyes for a moment, as if searching not for an answer, but for the silence in which the answer already lived. When he opened them, his gaze was soft, like moonlight on water—calm, clear, and deeply reflective.

He did not speak immediately.

Instead, he looked toward an old villager seated nearby—a man whose hands trembled slightly but whose eyes burned with clarity. Then toward an old woman, whose spine was curved like a question mark, but whose presence felt like an exclamation of grace. He gestured subtly toward them and began—not with explanation, but with a **poem** that felt more like a prayer, a song that reached not just the ears, but the marrow of the young listeners.

"Child, he is not an old man, worthless nor a burden,

He is a man rich in experience, a beacon to discern.

He is not tired, but tireless in spirit,

Not merely a person, but purity with clarity, a merit.

He is not a burden; he carries the family's weight,

A pillar of strength, guiding with wisdom innate.

Child, he should not be the last in your sight,

He is the first, illuminating your path with his light.

Learn this truth: a house without elders,
Is like a tree without leaves, a hollow shelter.
A home without them, like a butterfly without its hues,
A peacock without its dance, lost in the blues.

A tree without branches, leaves stripped away,
Child, for what you are today, their sacrifices lay.
From birth to death, from womb to grave,
Their love and sacrifice, like waves, endlessly brave.

From cradle to mortuary box, every word you utter,
Every breath, every rush, every dream, and flutter,
Is built upon the sacrifices they've made,
A testament to their love, in every facet displayed.

Remember, child, their legacy is your foundation,
Honour their presence, and their tireless dedication.
For in their wisdom, your future finds its grace,
In their sacrifices, your life's embrace."

When the last word faded into the hush, the banyan leaves rustled as though stirred by something greater than the wind. Some were with wet eyes, others with quiet awe. Even the elders bowed their heads slightly—not out of shame, but out of remembrance.

And then Guruji spoke—not to preach, but to reflect, as if offering a mirror:

Guruji said, turning to Vasudevan, "We do not rediscover the sacredness of the old through rituals alone. We rediscover it by slowing down long enough to see—really see—the ones who carried us before we could walk. The ones who waited without reward, who held the family together like the roots of this tree—quiet, hidden, yet essential."

He paused, then added:

"When we listen to their stories with our full heart, we are not going backwards—we are returning to what never left. For it is not the new that makes us wise, but the old that teaches us how to live with grace."

Aditi, who had been fidgeting with the hem of her dupatta for a while now, leaned forward. Her young face carried both curiosity and a quiet urgency, like a flower trying to bloom before dusk. Her voice was soft but sure:

"Guruji," she asked, **"what can the presence of elders teach us that words and books often cannot?"**

For a moment, the only sound was the rustle of leaves above them, as if the banyan tree itself had drawn a breath in anticipation.

Guruji turned to her slowly, his gaze resting not just on her face, but on the child within her question. His eyes glistened—not with tears, but with a kind of moist remembrance, like monsoon clouds holding stories that had never been written.

He said nothing at first.

Instead, he looked toward an old man seated nearby—his hand trembling as he fed rice to a crow perched boldly beside him. He then turned his gaze toward an elderly woman braiding her granddaughter's hair, her fingers weaving through generations as if they were threads of time.

And then Guruji spoke—not to explain, but to evoke.

"Child," he began, "a book may show you the recipe, but a grandmother's hand shows you how much love to add. A scripture can describe compassion, but watch an old man wipe the tears of a child—and you will feel what no verse can fully hold."

"Elders are not just people," he continued, "they are living archives—breathing libraries of the unspoken. Their wrinkles are not marks of decay, but of endurance. Each crease is a line from a story that chose to live, rather than be told."

He paused, letting the silence deepen. Then, his voice dropped, as a whisper meant for the soul:

"Have you ever noticed, how a river does not speak, yet the land remembers its touch? Elders are like that river—silent, but shaping. You may not remember every word they spoke, but you will carry the warmth of their gaze, the firmness of their hands, the shelter of their silence."

"Books can teach you facts," he said gently, "but presence… presence transmits wisdom like the scent of a flower carried by wind. You cannot catch it—but it enters you. You inhale it. And one day, when you're lost or broken, it will return—not as knowledge, but as a knowing."

Aditi's eyes shimmered—not with answers, but with something deeper: **recognition**. Of her ageing grandfather's silent smile. Of her grandmother's way of folding clothes as if wrapping prayers. Of stories never told aloud but etched in everyday gestures.

Guruji looked at her and smiled, finishing softly:

"The presence of elders is not there to instruct you. It is there to transform you—slowly, subtly, like sunlight turning fruit sweet. You may not notice it today. But one day, when you face life's storm, you will find their presence inside you—like roots holding the tree."

And in that moment, the garden was not just a place.

It became a temple of remembrance, where age was not weakness, but sacred architecture; where elders were not shadows of the past, but torches lighting the way forward.

CHAPTER III

He Who Plants a Tree

"Greatness is often planted in silence and watered with patience. Its roots grow deep in the soil of surrender."

– Shree Shambav

On a warm, honey-gold morning, the sun rose like a silent witness over the hills, touching everything with a promise. The village still yawned in slumber, but Sahasrananda—the monk whose silence often spoke more than sermons—was already walking. His robes stirred gently in the breeze, a soft rustle like the whisper of a prayer.

He walked not toward the temple or banyan grove, but to the edge of the village—a patch of dry, cracked earth where nothing grew anymore. It was land long abandoned, dismissed by most as lifeless. But to Sahasrananda, it was sleeping, not dead.

Behind him followed a small band of children and a few curious elders. The children laughed at first, chasing butterflies and skipping over stones, until they saw the monk kneel. There, in the centre of the barren ground, he dug—not with urgency, but with reverence, as if unearthing a forgotten memory.

From his robe, he gently took out a single fragile sapling, its roots wrapped in damp cloth, as if cradled by time. He placed it into the soil, covered it with earth, and pressed down softly—like tucking a child into bed.

The children stood still now, puzzled. "Will it grow?" one asked. "Why here?" another wondered.

Sahasrananda only smiled—a smile that felt like sunrise meeting dew—but said nothing. His silence was not empty; it was a seed waiting to bloom.

Days turned to weeks.

The children, once uncertain, began returning each morning. Something about that small act—the planting, the silence—had taken root in them too. They brought water in clay pots and carefully poured it at the base. They used sticks and old cloth to form a barrier, shielding it from goats. When others passed by and laughed, they spoke up: "Please don't step here—it's sacred."

They didn't know why, but they believed.

Old Ramesh brought ash from his hearth to nourish the soil. Padma began humming ancient songs near the sapling, as if coaxing its spirit to rise. What began as an act of planting had become an act of remembrance.

And though the sapling had not yet grown tall, something else had.

The land, once forgotten, was now visited daily. Conversations softened there. Laughter returned. The children no longer ran through it—they tiptoed. Even the wind seemed to move more slowly through that space, as if listening.

In truth, the sapling had already begun to grow—not just in soil, but in consciousness.

The monk had planted more than a tree—he had planted faith.

He had reminded them that even the most barren places—whether in land or heart—still hold the potential for life. That presence and care, given silently and consistently, can awaken the sacred, even where hope once felt impossible.

And he had taught—without ever uttering the words—that the future is not built by sermons shouted from rooftops, but by hands that dig, hearts that wait, and children who return.

Sujitha's eyes glistened with a tenderness she could no longer hold in. She was young, but her heart carried the weight of watching her father plant trees that would never bear fruit in his lifetime. She remembered him digging under the sun, quietly, patiently, with cracked hands and calloused hope. She would often ask, "Appa, why this effort? Will we even be here to enjoy the shade?" And he would simply smile and say, "Some things we do not do for ourselves, but for those we may never meet."

Now, standing before the monk with that same question burning in her chest, she gently asked, "Guruji, how often do we act with faith in a future we may not witness—and what does that say about the depth of our love?"

Shatananda did not answer immediately. He looked out over the garden where the sapling swayed slightly in the morning breeze, a fragile promise planted in uncertain soil. Around it, the children had built a small barrier of sticks and stones—an act of silent protection. A butterfly landed softly on one of its tiny leaves.

Then, he turned back to Sujitha, his eyes shimmering like still water catching the first rays of dawn.

"Child," he said gently, "to love without expectation of return is the rarest form of devotion. To plant what you may never harvest… to build what you may never live in… to sing a lullaby for an unborn child—this is love stretched beyond the borders of time."

He paused, his gaze sinking inward.

"The tree does not eat its own fruit. The river does not drink its own water. Yet they give endlessly. This is what the heart remembers when the mind forgets: That true love is not proven by gain, but by giving—quietly, anonymously, selflessly."

He placed his hand on the earth beside the sapling, "Every act of love toward a future unseen is a silent prayer woven into the roots of time. It is the soul's way of saying, I was here—not to take, but to give."

A soft breeze stirred. The children, who had grown quiet, looked around as if something sacred had just passed through them.

And then Sam, moved by the stillness, asked his question…

Sam, always the quiet observer. But this time, his voice carried a different weight—not of doubt, but of sincere wonder. The question had been growing in him for days, like a silent seed waiting for rain. His hands, calloused from helping his mother in the fields, now rested on his lap—gentle, still, like soil prepared for planting.

Looking up at the old monk, Sam asked softly, "Guruji, what are the seeds in your life that need planting today, even if the harvest is far beyond your time?"

The monk, Shatananda, slowly turned his gaze toward the distance—where a sapling, barely two feet tall, danced gently in the morning breeze. He let the question settle, like a sacred mist over a field at dawn.

Then, with a voice as calm as flowing water, he replied:

"Child… the greatest seeds are the ones we plant with no expectation of seeing their bloom. The seed of compassion, planted in a stranger's heart. The seed of courage, whispered into the ear of someone who may not believe in themselves yet. The seed of truth is offered even when it is inconvenient or forgotten by time.

I plant stories, Sam—not just words, but living stories. I plant them in your hearts, in silence, with the hope that someday, when you stand at the edge of despair or uncertainty, something in you will bloom without knowing why. That bloom—that clarity—is the harvest."

He picked up a fallen leaf, brown and crumpled. “You see this leaf? It once swayed green and full of life, drawing sunlight into its veins. And now, it returns to the earth—not as waste, but as nourishment. Even in its death, it feeds the soil for tomorrow’s bloom. That, too, is a seed.”

The elder paused, looking into Sam’s eyes with tenderness.

“We may never know who will sit in the shade of the tree we plant. We may never hear the laughter echoing in the home we helped build. But to plant with love—that is enough. To act without needing applause or reward—that is purity. And to give of yourself in ways that only the future will understand—that is the greatest offering one soul can make to another.”

Sam lowered his eyes, touched not with sorrow but with reverence. He understood now: that true legacy is not built in monuments or fame, but in unseen acts—small, sacred, selfless.

Sam lowered his eyes, touched not with sorrow but with reverence. He understood now: that true legacy is not built in monuments or fame, but in unseen acts—small, sacred, selfless.

Just then, Aadhya, a wide-eyed child with a voice full of wonder, leaned forward and asked, "Guruji, what does one truly plant when planting a tree?"

The monk's eyes lit with a gentle smile as he began to recite:

Then Aadhya, an inquisitive child, asked—

"What does one plant when planting a tree?"

The Master paused, his eyes grew kind,

"More than the roots the eye can see.

He plants a friend to sky and earth,

A bond of breath, of life and birth."

"He plants a song upon the breeze,

A dance within the autumn leaves.

He builds a tower touched by grace,

That offers shade in every place.

He paints the hills in living green,

And cools the air where hearts have been."

"He plants a bush of twilight peace,

Where birds begin their soft release—

A cradle built of branch and nest,

Where weary wings may come to rest.

He plants the bush that heals the day,
In rustling hymn and silent sway."
"He teaches strength in bowing low,
When stormy winds begin to blow.

In bending, not in breaking, true—
The tallest trees the storms live through.
He plants not just for his own eyes,
But for tomorrow's soft sunrise."

"He plants for rain, for bud and seed,
For every silent, growing need.
He draws the bees, the birds, the air,
And hosts the smallest lives with care.
He offers shade, he offers food,
Expecting nothing, yet doing good."

"He plants the roots that weave below,
Where secret life begins to grow.
They cradle earth in soft embrace,
And hold the hills in rooted grace.
They drink the waste we throw away,
And give the poison back as clay."

"He plants the glory of the land,
With open heart and quiet hand.
From child to elder, bird to bee,
He is a shelter, wide and free.
He holds the peace of plain and wood—
And sows it deep in brotherhood."

"And when you ask, 'But why, and who?'
Know this: he plants for me and you.
He plants in bark and sap and root,
A prayer without a word or flute.
A nation's soul, from sea to sea,
Is stirred in one who plants a tree."

A hush settled over the children and elders alike—not from silence, but from something deeper: understanding. They no longer saw the sapling as just a tree, but as a quiet cathedral of future blessings. In that moment, even the breeze seemed to listen.

CHAPTER IV

Why Meditation?

"Meditation is not an escape from life but a return to its centre—where your soul meets the sky within."

– Shree Shambav

The morning sun painted golden threads across the sleepy village, its light weaving gently through the leaves. In the small garden behind the ashram, children ran barefoot, their laughter ringing like temple bells in the wind. Nearby, a few elders quietly tended to the soil—watering young plants, clearing dry leaves, placing small stones to guide the water's path. Their movements were slow, deliberate, yet full of devotion—as if every act of gardening was a prayer returned to the earth.

Among them was a young boy—restless, curious, always questioning. Drawn by a quiet he didn't understand, he followed the footsteps of Sahasrananda, the silent monk whose presence was both soothing and strange. The boy trailed behind him along the winding path that led to the edge of the village, where an old neem tree stood like a sentinel of stillness.

There, beneath its vast, watchful shade, the monk sat down. His legs folded, his spine straight, his face calm as the sky before dawn. He closed his eyes—not in sleep, but in a depth beyond waking.

The boy, puzzled, sat a short distance away. At first, he was restless. He kicked dust into the air, made shapes with his fingers, drew uneven circles in the dirt. He threw pebbles. He whistled. But still, the monk did not move.

Time passed, though the boy did not know how much. Something was changing—not outside, but inside him. The noise within him—the chatter, the need to do, to understand, to act—began to quiet. The birds kept singing, the wind rustled gently through the neem leaves, and the sun climbed higher, casting dappled shadows on the earth. Yet the monk remained still, and so, eventually, did the boy.

He had never seen someone do nothing, yet seem so full.

Later, his curiosity resurfaced, now softer. He turned to Aadhya, the elder girl sitting nearby, and whispered, "What is he doing all this time?"

Aadhya smiled. Not with mockery, but with the warmth of someone who had once asked the same question.

"Meditation," she said gently.

The boy tilted his head. "But what is meditation?"

Aadhya paused, then said, "Come, let's ask Guruji."

They approached the monk together. As if sensing them, Sahasrananda slowly opened his eyes. They held no surprise, only presence—as if he had been with them all along, even in silence.

The boy repeated his question.

The monk's voice was soft, almost like the wind itself had formed words: "I was listening to the space between my thoughts."

The boy looked puzzled. But something in the monk's tone settled in his chest like a seed.

The boy's eyes blinked in wonder, but Aadhya, still curious and filled with longing to understand, knelt beside the monk and softly asked—

"But Guruji… what does meditation truly mean?"

Then Aadhya, an inquisitive child, asked—

"What does meditation truly mean?

Why must one sit with closed eyes tight,

When outside glows with golden light?"
The Master, hearing, gave no reply—
But silence deepened in his eye.

Again she asked, her voice a stream:
"Why meditate—what is this dream?"
The Master smiled, his presence still,
And answered soft with soul and will:
"It is the art of being near—
To all you are, when thoughts grow clear."

Meditation, child, is quiet grace,
A turning inward, soft embrace—
To see the thoughts like clouds drift by,
Yet not be caught, nor ask them why.
You watch the mind, then let it be,
Returning to the now—set free.
Not control, but gentle gaze—
A quiet flame within the haze.
You don't command, but sit as a friend—
With self and shadow, end to end.
In silence vast, you'll come to know

The roots of all that moves and grows.

The little boat of stillness sways,
On moonlit tides of dreamlike bays—
It journeys far to realms unseen,
Where starlight cloaks the in-between.
It drifts through lands with no known name,
Where peace and wonder are the same.

The people there are made of light,
Of laughter, waves, and morning bright—
They do not trade in gold or jade,
But in the songs the sea has made.
They do not chase the bloom or spring,
They are the joy such moments bring.

Their hearts are blue as endless skies,
Their voices rise like seabird cries.
The boat arrives, the gates unfold,
They greet me not with gems or gold—
But take my hands, and softly say,
"Come live with us, and drift away."

Yet I return—my love still near,
For in her arms, the stars appear.
I'd build a heaven on her chest,
And let the cosmos bless the rest.
The waves, moon-colored, sing and glide,
As jade and grasses dance in the tide.

And so, dear child, you ask me why—
Why one must sit and close the eye.
Let me explain through gentle song,
What draws the silent soul along:
Each reason shines, a guiding star—
To show you who you truly are.

To find a peace in noisy days—
A silence deep, a sacred space.
To hear the witness soft within,
And let the outer hush begin.
Awareness grows where stillness stays,
And lights the soul in subtle ways.

To heal the heart—release the weight,

Let grief dissolve, and ease its fate.
In silence, pain no longer clings—
Compassion comes on gentle wings.
The past, once sharp, begins to fade—
As love steps in, unafraid.

To train the mind, like calming rain,
Or taming thought's untamed terrain.
With practice, focus blooms anew,
Clarity, strength, and wisdom too.
Resilience deepens like the sea—
And thought becomes your symphony.

To touch the vastness, soul unbound,
Where sacred truths in stillness sound.
Beyond the form, beyond the name,
You meet the self that none can tame.
In meditation's open door,
You meet the one you've been before.

And finally—to live, not drift,
To root the soul, to feel the lift.
Not to escape, but to arrive,

Where presence makes the world alive.

The now becomes your sacred ground,

Where breath and joy are ever found.

The boy sat quietly, his fidgeting forgotten. He didn't understand every word—but he felt them, like warm sunlight through his skin.

Others smiled, their eyes misty, and whispered, "Maybe that's what meditation feels like… like listening with the heart."

Sahasrananda continued, his voice like a river flowing slowly through stone: "Just as music lives not only in notes but in the silence between them, so too does wisdom arise in the space between thoughts. Meditation is not about doing—it is about being. It is listening to life not through ears, but through awareness. Most people hear the noise of their mind. But in silence, we begin to hear the truth beneath the noise."

The boy looked up at the leaves dancing in the light. He didn't fully understand, but for the first time, he didn't need to.

He sat down beside the monk again—not to wait, not to fidget, not to ask—but simply to be.

Medha's voice had not been loud, yet it seemed to ripple through the garden like a soft wind brushing the still surface of a pond.

"Guruji, what lies beneath our thoughts when we allow ourselves to simply be—without judgment, noise, or doing?"

Sahasrananda did not answer at once.

He simply looked up—at the old neem tree above him, its gnarled branches stretching into the soft blue, leaves trembling in the hush of dawn. A squirrel darted across a branch. A bird called once and fell silent again. Around them, the world did not rush. It listened.

Then, softly, Guruji spoke—his voice like the rustling of dry leaves, gentle yet anchored by lifetimes of stillness.

"Beneath our thoughts, child, lies the ocean beneath the waves.

Most live on the surface—all foam and motion, all stories and storms. But when you stop paddling… when you let the wind pass through you without resistance… You begin to descend.

And there, in the quiet beneath thinking, is not emptiness—but vastness.

A silence that doesn't lack—it contains. A presence that is not 'you' in the usual way, yet it is more you than you've ever known.

It is like the space between heartbeats—without it, there would be no rhythm, no song of life.

It is the ground beneath all noise, the canvas behind every painting, the sky in which all clouds appear and disappear.

When you learn to be still—not by force, but by trust—this hidden ground of Being reveals itself."

He closed his eyes for a moment, as if remembering something too sacred for speech.

Then he continued, more gently still:

"When you rest in that space, you are not broken, not becoming, not lacking. You are no longer a river searching for the sea.

You are the sea itself.

You don't have to understand it. You only need to be with it.

Like the moon doesn't chase reflection—it simply shines, and the lake receives its light."

Medha didn't speak. Her eyes shimmered—not from understanding, but from sensing something beyond thought. Something that stirred like morning light touching the petals of a half-opened flower.

And in that stillness, where no answer was loud, the question itself dissolved—like a drop into the ocean it had been searching for.

The question settled in the air like incense curling through a quiet temple.

Apoorva's voice had come gently, not seeking to impress, but to touch. Around her, the garden held its breath—the sound of birdsong softened, even the rustling of trees seemed to pause, as though the very earth leaned in to listen.

"Guruji, can silence reveal truths that words often fail to express? What happens when we stop trying to understand and simply observe?"

Sahasrananda slowly turned to face her, his eyes deep with that ancient tenderness only those who have befriended silence truly carry. A faint smile touched his lips—not one of amusement, but recognition.

He gestured for her to sit beside him. A moment passed in quietude. No words, only the rustling wind brushing through leaves. Then, softly, he began to speak—not to answer, but to reveal.

"Have you ever watched the moonrise over still waters?" he asked, eyes fixed on the horizon as if remembering it himself.

"When the moon appears, it doesn't explain its light—it simply reflects across the surface. The lake does not ask questions; it only becomes still, and in that stillness, it receives the full beauty of the moon."

"That is silence, Apoorva. A mirror without ripples. And in that mirror, truth does not need a name."

He paused and pointed to a butterfly resting on a marigold.

"Look at that. Had I tried to speak of its colours, I'd steal more than I gave. But in silence, it tells you everything."

Then he shared a story—one from his youth, when he, too, had sought answers through words and logic.

"When I was a young seeker, I once climbed to a remote monastery in the Himalayas to meet a sage known only as 'The Listener.' He had not spoken for over thirty years.

I sat before him and asked, 'What is the highest truth?'

He said nothing. Only looked at me.

Hours passed. The snow fell outside. A candle flickered in the dim cave. I grew restless, then angry, then exhausted.

But somewhere in that silence… something broke open. Not in my mind, but in my being.

And I understood—not as a concept, but as a presence.

That the answer I sought was not hidden in complexity—it was hidden behind the noise within me."

His voice grew softer, more intimate.

"Apoorva, some truths are like the scent of rain on dry earth. You cannot write it down, but you know it in your bones.

Silence is not the absence of communication—it is the most honest form of it.

When you stop trying to grasp, the truth slips quietly into your open palm.

When you stop trying to name, the sacred whispers its real name."

Apoorva looked down, her hand resting on the warm earth.

She did not speak. She did not need to.

For some truths are not meant to be heard—they are meant to be felt, when the heart finally listens in silence.

CHAPTER V

Embracing Life's Flow

"Do not seek to shape life like clay—be shaped like water, and you will never break."

– Shree Shambav

The storm came without warning—dark clouds swelling like an angry ocean in the sky. Wind howled through the narrow paths of the village like a beast unchained. Children were ushered inside, cattle herded into sheds, windows shuttered. The sky cracked open with lightning, and the earth trembled under its roar. Fear hung thick in the air.

But outside, beyond the panic, Sahasrananda knelt in the garden. His robe clung to his skin, soaked by rain, yet he moved gently among the trembling plants. He secured the saplings with soft ropes, whispered mantras under his breath, and sang to the storm as though it were a guest, not an enemy. His hands did not rush. His eyes did not flinch. He worked with the storm, not against it.

The village elder, Parthiban, watched from his window. He could barely believe the sight—this calm man, in the eye of a hurricane, tending to flowers while the world seemed to fall apart.

Days later, when the skies had cleared and the sun returned with its golden warmth, Parthiban walked to the garden. The damage was minimal. The plants, though bent, had not broken. Sahasrananda was now sweeping fallen leaves with the same gentle focus, as if the storm had only been another passerby.

The elder, still puzzled, finally asked, "Guruji, how can you be so calm amid so much chaos? How does one hold such stillness while the world shakes?"

Sahasrananda paused, looked toward the river in the distance, and then back at the elder. His eyes carried the stillness of someone who had learned to listen beyond sound.

He smiled and said softly, "Like a river, life flows through both storm and sun. One must flow, not fight. To resist the current is to drown. But to trust the flow is to be carried—even through thunder."

The sky had cleared after days of storm. Yet in many hearts, the turbulence lingered.

One evening, under the neem tree where villagers often gathered in the soft hush of twilight, Samriddhi sat quietly beside Guruji, her eyes reflecting something unsettled. She had always been strong—fierce in responsibility, sharp in mind—but recently, life had overwhelmed her. Her father's illness, a failed harvest, and the crumbling of dreams she had nurtured for years. Control, once her armour, had slipped through her fingers.

"Guruji," she asked, her voice barely more than a whisper, "How can we learn to surrender when life turns turbulent—when everything within us wants to resist what we cannot change?"

Sahasrananda looked toward the horizon where the last rays of the sun kissed the mountains, golden and soft. He let the silence stretch like a deep breath before he spoke—not in haste, but in presence.

He then began a story.

The Bamboo and the Oak

"There were once two trees that stood on the edge of a forest," Guruji said. "An old oak—tall, proud, unwavering. And beside it, a bamboo—thin, supple, swaying in every breeze.

When the storm came, it roared like a wild beast, tearing through the forest with fury. The oak stood firm, chest out, determined to withstand it. But the wind was stronger. It snapped branches, tore bark, and finally, with one mighty gust, it uprooted the oak.

And yet, the bamboo remained. It bent, it bowed low, nearly touched the earth—but it did not break. When the storm passed, the bamboo stood upright again, untouched at its core.

Why? Because it knew how to surrender."

The Deeper Meaning

Guruji turned to Samriddhi. "You see, surrender is not defeat. It is wisdom. It is knowing the difference between what we can hold and what we must release. It is trusting the rhythm of the river, even when we don't see the ocean it flows to."

He continued gently, "You were taught to control—to strive, to achieve, to fix everything. That has its place. But when life becomes a storm, that very control becomes your cage. To surrender is to open the door. It is to stop fighting the waves and learn to float. You do not drown by surrendering. You drown by resisting what is already here."

Samriddhi's eyes welled up—not from pain, but from recognition. She saw how her clinging, her resistance, her desperate need to fix everything had only deepened her suffering. And in Guruji's words, she felt not rebuke, but release.

"You are not meant to carry the whole sky," he said. "You are only meant to open to it."

Sahasrananda said, "Surrender begins not with action, but with awareness. It is the quiet realisation: 'I am not the storm; I am the sky in which the storm passes.' When we accept this, not as an idea but as an experience, life begins to soften. Even pain begins to reveal its teachings. We stop asking 'Why me?' and begin to ask, "What is life trying to show me?"

To surrender is not to give up—it is to give in to something greater. It is the soul bowing before the mystery, saying: "I do not understand, but I am willing to trust."

The fire had nearly died down. Embers glowed gently as the villagers sat under the night sky, stars shimmering like forgotten memories. Pavitra, her eyes fixed on the flickering orange light, broke the silence.

"Guruji," she asked, "what does it truly mean to trust life's river… especially when we don't know where it's flowing? When the path ahead is fogged in uncertainty, and our feet tremble?"

The monk looked at her with a kindness so still, it felt like the pause between two breaths of the universe.

The Boat and the River

He began softly.

"Long ago," Guruji said, "a young man set out in search of a mythical village—one said to lie beyond seven rivers and three shadowed forests. It held no maps, only legends. Everyone who'd gone before him either turned back or disappeared into the silence of unknowing.

But this young man was different—his heart whispered not of arrival, but of longing.

He built a small wooden boat, said goodbye to all he knew, and let the river guide him.

There were days of calm and songs of birds. And then days when storms wept from the sky and the river thrashed like a wounded beast. He cried out many times, "Why won't you show me the way?"

But the river never answered in words.

Only later did he realise—the river was the way.

One night, exhausted and unsure, he dreamed of an old sage on the riverbank who said, 'The river knows the shape of your soul better than you do. Trust it—not to take you where you want to go, but to carry you where you're meant to grow.'"

Sahasrananda paused, "Pavitra, to trust life's river is to place your heart in the current of the unknown. It is to surrender your demand for clarity and trade it for presence. Not because the path is easy, but because the compass is within.

When you float in faith, even the fog becomes sacred. Even not-knowing becomes a form of wisdom.

It's only when we loosen our grip on control that we begin to feel the hands of grace guiding us."

Sahasrananda looked into her eyes.

"We want guarantees—signposts, explanations, certainty. But life is not a highway with exit boards. It is a river. And rivers bend. Sometimes they appear to go backwards only to gather momentum for the next leap. Sometimes they carve canyons, other times they nourish fields. But they always flow toward the ocean—toward wholeness."

"Trusting life's river doesn't mean you never fear. It means you feel the fear, and you still step in."

"It means you stop asking, 'Where is this going?' And start asking, 'How deeply can I be here?'"

Guruji turned to the group with a soft smile and recited a verse:

A wise man asked, "Why are you angry and torn?

My child, what sorrow have you silently borne?"

As if you have lost everything you ever had,

Why do you look so gloomy and sad?"

Every problem has a solution, my dear,

No trouble exists without a way to clear.

Life is like a wheel, turning round and round,

With inevitable ups and downs.

If you were happy without knowing sadness,

How would you appreciate the beauty of gladness?

We must sail through rough waves, it's true,

To finally reach the shore safe and new.

Accept the path as it treads before you,

Don't try to change anything or anyone, too.

Just embrace what comes, with an open heart,

For in time, you will understand each part.

Life is a flow, my child, let it take you along,

In accepting the truth, you'll find you belong.

Once you accept and see life's truth and grace,

You'll celebrate each moment, in every place.

Each step you take, each breath you draw,

Will be a testament to life's awe.

For in the dance of joy and sorrow,

You'll find hope and strength for tomorrow.

So, my child, let go of anger and dread,

Embrace life's flow, and look ahead.

For in acceptance lies true peace,

And in that peace, life's wonders never cease.

Sahasrananda looked at Pavitra and said, "Sometimes, poems hold the silence between truths. Let them carry you across the rivers you fear."

Pavitra closed her eyes. Something inside her—a tight knot of waiting—began to loosen.

She no longer needed to know the entire path. She just needed to take the next step with courage and let the river hold the rest.

CHAPTER VI

The Eternal Stillness

"True stillness isn't silence outside—it's serenity within, even when the world trembles."

– *Shree Shambav*

Jahnavi was known in the village not for her loudness, but for her listening. She moved like early morning mist—soft, quiet, unnoticed by many, yet present in every corner. A seeker not of answers, but of essence, she carried an old sorrow within her—something never spoken, something that made her voice softer and her gaze deeper. While others came to Sahasrananda with questions about doing, she came with questions about being.

The Storm Within

It had been a week since the monsoon storm had torn through the village. Roofs had been blown off, trees uprooted, and hearts left unsettled. But even after the winds had died, something within Jahnavi continued to stir restlessly. It wasn't fear of the storm outside—it was the storm inside. The kind that no one sees. The one that brews in silence.

She found Sahasrananda one morning, seated by the old riverbend where the water flowed gently again, as if nothing had happened. He sat with eyes closed, his palms resting upward on his knees, his spine straight, his breath calm—like a mountain unmoved by weather.

She bowed and sat near him. After a long silence, she finally asked, her voice quivering slightly:

"Sahasrananda, in the storms of our life, where do we find our stillness? Is there a space within us untouched by external turmoil?"

Sahasrananda slowly opened his eyes. They held the colour of rain-washed earth—deep, steady, and ancient.

He looked at her, not with pity, but with presence.

"Let me tell you a story," he said gently, "of a lake I once visited high in the Himalayas."

"It was surrounded by storms—clouds roared above, winds howled through the cliffs. But when I reached its edge, I saw something that has never left me. Beneath the ripples on the surface, there was a stillness so pure, so untouched, that even the storm could not reach it. The surface danced, yes, but the depths… the depths remained undisturbed."

He paused, letting the words sink in.

"You, Jahnavi, are not the storm. You are the lake. And the storm may pass over your surface—but in the sanctuary of your being, in that sacred space where breath meets silence, there lies a stillness that nothing can touch. To find it, you don't need to fight the storm. You need only dive deep enough."

"Stillness," he continued, "is not the absence of movement—it is the presence of awareness. Like the eye of a hurricane—calm, centred, surrounded by fury—there is an inner eye in all of us, a space untouched by the noise of the world. Meditation is not escape—it is remembrance. A return to the part of you that was never disturbed."

"And once you've touched that place, Jahnavi, even when you return to the surface of life, something inside you remains unshaken. You carry the silence with you—not as silence of speech, but the silence of fear, the silence of need."

Sahasrananda gently placed a flower petal on the water's surface. They both watched it float.

"The world will always bring waves," he whispered. "But you are not the waves. You are the water."

Hitesh was a man shaped not by triumphs, but by the tender bruises of life. The quiet observer in every room, he rarely spoke—, but when he did, it came from a place of deep seeing. Years of inner inquiry had taught him that strength was not about dominance, but about endurance, humility, and presence. Watching Sahasrananda calmly tend the garden as the storm raged had left an imprint on his soul—one that could not be erased by time or logic. That image became a question that stirred in his heart like an unanswered prayer. And so, seated under the shade of the old banyan, Hitesh voiced what many had felt, but few had dared to ask.

Hitesh's Question:

"Sahasrananda, what if true strength is not loud or forceful—but silent, centred, and unwavering like the monk under the storm?"

Sahasrananda turned toward him, eyes filled with a knowing stillness, the kind that arises not from learning but from deep being. A breeze passed through the trees above, rustling the leaves like an invisible blessing.

"Hitesh," he said gently, "have you ever seen a great mountain in a storm? It does not roar back at the thunder. It simply stands. It absorbs the fury without resistance, because its roots are in silence, not sound."

He motioned toward a nearby stream, its waters gliding over pebbles with ease.

"Or consider the river. Is it weak because it yields? No. It flows because it understands—it is not here to conquer, but to arrive. To trust its path, even when it bends into the unknown, is a strength beyond comprehension."

He looked directly into Hitesh's eyes now, his voice softer but firmer.

"The world often confuses noise with power, action with authority. But true strength is quieter than all that. It is the presence that doesn't flinch. The breath that remains steady when everything else shakes. It is the warrior who doesn't draw his sword because he knows the battle is within."

He pointed toward his own chest.

"The monk in the storm did not resist the chaos—he simply remained who he was within it. That is why the storm could not touch him. Because he was rooted—not in control—but in truth."

He paused. A bird sang from a distant branch, and the silence after its note felt deeper than before.

"When a man becomes the eye of the storm, he doesn't need to run from it. Stillness is not escape—it is sovereignty."

Sahasrananda, after a pause, said, "Thunder may echo across mountains, but it is silence that endures beneath them. The wise do not raise their voice to be heard—they deepen their presence until the world listens."

Sahasrananda's words settled into the silence like petals falling on still water. No one spoke for a while. The truth did not need to be debated—it only needed to be received.

Hitesh bowed his head slightly, not in defeat, but in reverence. Somewhere in his heart, the winds had stilled.

As if the moment itself had something more to say, Sahasrananda gently whispered lines of verse—words not meant to instruct, but to awaken:

If you can empty your mind,

Like a river surrendering to the ocean,

You will find a stillness deeper than silence,

A tranquillity that hums with eternal devotion.

Amid the endless rush of worldly desires,

Pause, and watch them whirl, relentless streams.

Yet feel the pull of their quiet return,

To the Source, the cradle of all dreams.

Each being, like a leaf in autumn's fall,
Drifts back to the arms of its sacred start.
To return is not an ending but a call,
A peace that whispers deep within the heart.

To know this destiny is to perceive,
The rhythm of constancy, the eternal glow.
To feel the pulse of light, we must believe,
Enlightenment's path is the one to know.

Without this knowing, life becomes a shade,
A fleeting shadow, sorrowed and confined.
But union with the Source will never fade,
It frees the heart and liberates the mind.

When you touch the Divine, impartial you'll stay,
A noble surrender, untouched by fear.
Life's shifting tides no longer hold their sway,
For in that stillness, the truth is clear.

Life and loss, gain and grief, simply unfold,
As ripples across an infinite stream.
In oneness, the vast mysteries are told,

And consciousness awakens from its dream.

For in that knowing, you find what is true,
Not just peace, but the essence of design.
You are a reflection of the endless hue,
A spark of the eternal, wholly divine.

The air felt different after the final verse—as if each listener had touched the edge of something eternal.No longer was stillness a passive silence; it had become a sacred presence, a quiet strength echoing in every breath.

PART TWO

BLOOMS OF THE HEART

"True love warms and wounds—one flame teaches devotion, the other burns illusion."

- *Shree Shambav*

CHAPTER VII

Love: Crown and Crucifix

"The greatest loves are not those without struggle, but those that rise through it, hand in hand."

– Shree Shambav

The Radiance of Shatananda

In the quiet folds of the kingdom, a name began to stir across lips as a sacred hymn whispered from one heart to another—Shatananda. He was no ruler, no scholar famed in scrolls, no priest bound by rituals. And yet, his name moved with a mysterious power. It carried the softness of still water and the strength of unseen roots.

The villagers spoke of him not just with reverence, but with a kind of quiet wonder, as if his presence had somehow realigned the fabric of their lives. It was said he lived near the mountains in Kalpa village, where once barren soil now bloomed with rare flowers. Not planted, but willed into life, they said—through presence, not plough.

One day, the king of the land, driven by a desire to witness the true condition of his people, set forth disguised with his ministers. He wanted to know the heart of his kingdom—not through reports, but through dust on his feet and voices in the wind.

As they wandered through a humble village, the scent of wood smoke and grain hung in the air. They passed two elderly men sitting beneath a neem tree. The king, cloaked as a traveller, overheard a fragile voice, cracking not just with age but with pain.

"Since my son died," the old man said, "every day has become heavier than the last. Grief has made even the sunrise feel like a burden."

The other elder gently placed a hand on his friend's shoulder.

"Why don't you go to Kalpa? Go see Shatananda. People say even silence speaks through him. He does not give answers, but hearts return lighter."

The king turned to his minister.

"Who is this Shatananda?"

The minister, after a thoughtful pause, replied,

"Your Majesty, I've heard whispers. He is a monk who came years ago and made his home near the mountains. They say he turned cracked earth into a garden—not with water, but with stillness. His presence alone makes things grow."

The king said nothing, but something within him stirred. As they continued through the marketplace, amidst the cries of vendors and clatter of wheels, the name rose again and again, carried on the wings of everyday conversations.

By the time they returned to the palace, the king was curious to know more about Shatananda.

Beneath the Banyan Tree

Far away in Kalpa, Shatananda sat as always beneath the old Banyan tree. Its thick roots coiled into the earth like ancient serpents of wisdom, its canopy wide enough to shade seekers from the sun—and sometimes, from themselves.

That day, the air smelled of rain and longing. People had gathered, not for miracles, but for meaning.

Among them came Mira and Dev, a young couple once radiant with love, now dimmed by friction and unmet expectations. Their hands no longer reached easily. Their words, once a song, now often clashed like mismatched notes.

Mira knelt before the monk, tears heavy in her eyes.

"Why does love feel like both a blessing and a burden?" she whispered. "It lifted me once. Now it wears me down."

Shatananda listened—not with urgency, but with the stillness of a mountain listening to a passing storm.

Then, without speaking, he pointed to two vines climbing an old stone pillar beside the tree. One vine was soft and flowering, the other thick with thorns. Yet they grew together—wrapped around the same support, neither dominating the other.

"Love," the monk finally spoke, "is both crown and crucifix. It will lift you in ecstasy and pierce you with pain. Not because it is flawed, but because it calls you to grow."

He told them a parable:

"Long ago, two stars fell in love. One gave light, the other warmth. They longed to be close, but every time they neared, their intensity burned. So they learned—not to collide, but to co-exist, sharing the sky without swallowing each other. Their love lit the night not by possession, but by presence."

The couple sat in silence, the story carving space in their hearts. The tears did not stop—but now, they watered understanding, not sorrow.

They learned that to love is to surrender without losing oneself, and to stay even when the skies turn grey—not as sacrifice, but as sacred participation.

Mira said to herself, True love is not the absence of conflict but the presence of commitment through conflict. It teaches us that surrender is not weakness—it is a deeper strength, the kind that bows without breaking.

Mira lowered her eyes, her heart heavy yet strangely lifted. Dev held her hand—not to fix, but simply to stay. The silence that followed settled like golden dust over the clearing.

Then Aadhya, an inquisitive child, spoke with soft wonder, "Tell me more of love, so deep."

Shatananda's gaze turned to her, eyes aglow with tenderness. He did not speak right away. His expression softened—as though watching a star half-sleep, or hearing the echo of a memory too sacred for words. At last, his voice rose, slow and still, as if pulled from the depths where the soul drinks will.

And he recited:

Then Aadhya, an inquisitive child, asked—

"Tell me more of love, so deep."

The Master paused, his gaze turned soft,

As though he watched a star half-sleep.

At last, he spoke with breath drawn still,

From places where the soul drinks will:

"When love calls out, go where he leads,

Though thorn and cliff may line his path.

And when his wings enclose your frame,

Yield to his touch, both calm and wrath.

For hidden in his feathered grace,

May lie the blade that carves your place.

When love speaks, believe his voice,
Though it may break your cherished dreams.
Like winter's wind that strips the rose,
His truth may tear your garden's seams.
For love, in crowning, crucifies—
And lifts you only as he tries.

As much as love shall make you bloom,
So shall he prune with sharpened hand.
He climbs to kiss your sunlit leaves,
Then shakes the roots that clutch the land.
For what he gives is not in vain—
He sculpts joy through shaping pain.

Like sheaves of grain, he gathers near,
And strips the husks to find your core.
He grinds you white, then folds you slow,
And kneads your soul with ancient lore.
Then casts you to his sacred flame,
To rise anew in love's own name.

All this will love do unto you,
To bare the secrets that you keep.
And in that depth, a truth will bloom—
A piece of Life's own heart will weep.
But if you seek but love's delight,
Then flee the fire, avoid the night.

Step from love's threshing floor unseen,
Into a world both safe and still.
Their joy is half, and tears are dim,
And hearts forget their highest will.
Their laughter fades, and sorrow sleeps,
But nothing climbs the mountain's steeps.

Love gives but self, and takes the same,
It owns no thing, nor claims a right.
It seeks no chains, no promises—
It is its own eternal light.
To love is not to bind or hold,
But live within love's heart, untold.

Say not, 'God dwells within my soul,'
But rather, 'I in His abide.'

And think not you can guide love's stream—
It flows where only hearts can ride.
For love will steer, if you are true,
And chart a path designed for you.

Love has no goal but to be love,
Yet if you must hold some desire—
Let it be this: to melt and flow,
A singing stream that won't retire.
To feel too much, to break and mend,
To bleed with joy you'd still defend.

To rise each dawn with wings of thanks,
And bless the day with love's bright flame.
To sleep each night with sacred prayer,
Still whispering your lover's name.
To dream with peace, lips wrapped in praise,
And wake to love a thousand ways."

When the final words faded, the grove held its breath. Even the wind seemed hushed, as though not to disturb the silence love had left behind.

Diya was not one to speak often, but when she did, her words carried the weight of oceans. Young in age but old in reflection, she was known for her gentle presence and eyes that often looked not at people, but into them. She had lived quietly among the others in Kalpa village, always listening, always observing. Where others sought answers in scripture or speech, Diya sought them in silence, in nature, and in the movement of her own tender heart.

But there was one realm she feared to enter fully—love. Not because she hadn't felt it, but because she had. And in its aftermath, she had tasted both the sacredness and the sorrow it brings. It left in her a trembling reverence, like one who had touched fire and could still feel the warmth, long after the flames were gone.

A long pause lingered, and the silence grew thick like incense. Then came Diya's voice—fragile, honest, searching.

"Sahasrananda…" she said softly, her eyes moist but steady, "Can we hold love not just as joy, but also as a spiritual practice… one that humbles and transforms us?"

Shatananda's did not answer right away. Instead, he began to speak in a story:

"There once was a potter," Shatananda began, "who fell in love with the clay he shaped each morning. He would sit with it before sunrise, and whisper his dreams into its formlessness. Slowly, it became a bowl, a cup, a vase. But one day, a piece cracked in the kiln. The potter wept. He had poured his heart into it."

The villagers listened closely. Diya's eyes didn't leave his face.

"An old traveller came by and saw the broken pot. 'Why do you cry?' he asked. 'Because I loved it,' said the potter. The traveller smiled, 'Then let it teach you this: true love is not in the perfect shape, but in how you hold what is broken.'"

Shatananda looked directly at Diya.

"Yes, Diya," he said with a voice as soft as twilight rain, "Love is not merely an emotion—it is sadhana, a sacred discipline. It humbles because it strips the ego. It transforms because it demands truth. To love is not just to feel—it is to serve, to stay, to surrender."

He paused, then added,

"Love, like fire, does not leave you unchanged. If it doesn't burn away your pride, it hasn't yet become sacred. And if it doesn't deepen your compassion, you haven't yet touched its essence."

In the quiet that followed, the others began to reflect.

Diya sat with her palms open on her knees, as if receiving a deeper understanding—not just with her mind, but with her very breath.

Love, she realised, was not just the light that made her bloom, but also the soil that held her tears. It was the mountain path that challenged her, the mirror that showed her shadows, the wind that tore her illusions, and the rain that softened her into surrender.

To love another—truly—is to practice the art of vanishing ego, to bear witness without clinging, to be available without possession, and to walk with them not behind, not ahead, but beside—as two flames that warm, not consume.

After a long pause…

A gentle breeze stirred the leaves of the banyan tree under which Shatananda sat, his eyes half-closed as if listening to the wind speak. The air was thick—not with tension, but with expectancy. Those who gathered around him that day sensed something stirring, not in the world, but within themselves.

Bhavya was among them. She was known not for the loudness of her voice, but for the clarity of her spirit. Her presence was steady, like a lamp that never flickered—even in a storm. Once a teacher of philosophy in the capital, Bharati had come to Kalpa not for answers, but to unlearn. Life had handed her a series of relationships—beautiful, difficult, honest, and broken—and in their wake, she had begun to see that intellect alone could not mend what the heart carried.

That day, she sat with her hands folded in her lap, her voice calm but trembling with truth.

"Where," she asked, "have we confused control with connection in our relationships… and how might surrender open a deeper intimacy?"

Shatananda opened his eyes. He looked at her—not to examine, but to acknowledge. Then, in his way, he began not with an answer, but with a story.

"Let me tell you of the falcon and the wind," he said.

"Once, in a forest far from here, a falcon was born to soar. Its wings were strong, and its eyes sharp. But it grew up in a golden cage—a gift to a king who loved beauty but feared freedom. Each day, the falcon was fed the best meats, bathed in rose water, and sung to by musicians. And yet, it was restless.

One day, the cage was left open. The falcon hesitated. It had never known a sky beyond the window. But something ancient stirred in its blood.

It flew.

At first, the wind frightened it. The sky was too wide, the currents unpredictable. It longed for the comfort of the cage, where everything was known and safe. But then came a gust—wild, strong, untamed. The falcon surrendered to it, let go of the need to steer, and allowed itself to be carried.

And in that surrender, something shifted. It did not lose its way—it found its wings."

The listeners sat in silence, and Shatananda turned to Bharati.

"We often think love is about holding on tightly," he said. "About steering, managing, controlling, protecting. But control is fear disguised as care. Connection is not forged through grip—it is born in grace."

He continued:

"When we try to manage others—how they love, respond, or change—we are no longer meeting them, we are meeting our fear. Surrender is not letting go of the other—it is letting go of the illusion that we must shape them to keep them."

He looked gently at Bharati.

"To surrender is not to vanish—it is to be fully present without needing to possess. It is to replace 'How do I hold on to you?' with 'How can I meet you as you are, here and now?'"

The banyan leaves rustled above, and a few petals drifted down between them—light, effortless, unafraid of falling.

Bharati did not speak. She didn't need to. Her breath deepened, and her hands slowly opened in her lap—not to grasp, but to receive.

Somewhere deep within, she knew: real intimacy doesn't bloom in control, but in the vast and vulnerable field of surrender.

CHAPTER VIII

A True Love's Odyssey

"Some words, once written in love, carve themselves into the soul and never age."

– Shree Shambav

The monk sat in silence beneath the ancient banyan, its branches whispering memories older than time. Around him, the village stirred with quiet reverence. That morning, something sacred seemed to hover in the air—like the hush before a song that had not yet been sung.

An elderly woman approached slowly, leaning on a wooden cane. Her sari was simple, faded by time, and her silver hair was woven in a humble braid. But in her hands, she held something delicate and powerful—a folded, yellowed letter, soft from being opened too many times, smudged with fingerprints and tears.

Her name was Saraswati. Once the village's brightest singer, now a widow whose voice trembled not from age, but from a well of memories too deep to speak lightly.

She knelt before Shatananda, her knees aching but her eyes strong.

“I found this,” she said softly, offering the letter, “tucked in the folds of my wedding sari. It’s from him—from Devendra. He wrote it on the battlefield, thinking it would be his last.”

Her voice quivered. “But he returned. Bloodied, broken… but alive. We grew old together. Yet now… he’s gone beyond. But I feel him still. Even death couldn’t break what we shared.”

The monk took the letter gently, as though receiving a relic. He unfolded it and began to read—not quickly, not ceremoniously, but as though he were invoking something sacred, word by word. The villagers gathered, drawn not by curiosity but by the gravity of love rediscovered.

He paused often—not merely to catch his breath, but to allow the silence to speak. With each line, the battlefield gave way to the courtyard where Saraswati once waited, lamp in hand. Each sentence brought petals of the past into the light of now.

When the letter ended, the air hung full with unspoken feeling. Tears brimmed in Saraswati's eyes, but they no longer fell. They shimmered like dew before dawn.

Then, Shatananda turned to her and said gently, "Your story is not just a memory—it is music still playing across lifetimes. And that music has found its voice again." He handed her a parchment on which he had written a verse—his own heart's response to hers:

He recited:

I hear the celestial music from afar,
Though in darkness, I meditate on your grace,
Your melodies transport me into a trance,
In your thoughts, I find solace and embrace.

Your beauty and harmonies draw me near,
Curiosity fuels my desire to perceive,
As if I've known you since time's inception,
The more I listen, the more I want to receive,
Living within the realm of your thoughts is so dear.

In secrecy, you play your enchanting flute,
Each breath transformed into divine sound,
A melody that brings tranquillity and divinity,
Oh, dear flute, in essence, we are bound.

You yearn for the touch of his breath divine,
I long to behold him, to see him shine,
Our hearts echo the same longing deep within,

Yearning for the reunion of old reminiscences' sign,
Oh, dear flute, in essence, our desires align.

The melodies evoke tears in my eyes,
A poignant sadness stirs within my heart,
Pain and grief haunt me day by day,
Though close, we're kept apart,
Oh, Krishna, when will I hear your divine melodies arise?

Sleep evades me at this late hour's call,
Without you, my being feels incomplete,
What curse has befallen us, dear one?
Though near a vast distance, we meet,
Oh, Krishna, when shall we dance and enthral?

No medicine can soothe this ache I bear,
Oh, Krishna, I long for our times of yore,
To partake in the Ras dance beneath the silver moon,
Your melodies comfort me to my core,
I yearn for the music played from afar, to share.

As the last line faded, the leaves rustled as if applauding softly. Saraswati pressed the parchment to her chest, tears streaming down, not in grief—but in communion. Her love had become a prayer, a presence beyond absence.

Shatananda looked at the gathered crowd and spoke, not loudly, but with a gentleness that settled into every heart:

"This love is no longer just hers—it belongs to all hearts seeking eternity in time."

Saraswati rose slowly. As she turned to leave, a sudden breeze stirred the blossoms scattered at her feet. They lifted and danced for a moment in the air—just like the memories she carried, no longer bound to sorrow, but to song.

As the petals settled once more beneath the banyan tree, the silence returned—full, sacred, shimmering with aftertones of Saraswati's love and Shatananda's verse. It was the kind of silence that doesn't beg to be broken, but deepened.

Padmavathi sat quietly beside the monk. A gentle woman of quiet strength, she was known in the village for her wisdom and grace. Her husband had passed years ago, yet she never spoke of loss as absence. There was something in her that carried remembrance like a sacred song—soft but unceasing.

She turned toward the monk with eyes not heavy with grief, but lit with wonder, as if carrying a question that had lived in her long before words found it.

She asked slowly, her voice like the edge of a prayer, "Can love outlive the body and the spoken word—can it become an eternal rhythm echoing through the soul?"

Shatananda didn't answer right away.

Instead, he looked toward the river beyond the banyan grove, where the waters shimmered in the golden light of late afternoon. "Come," he said gently.

The small group followed as the monk walked down to the riverbank, where the current moved quietly—neither hurried nor still, a sacred in-between.

He pointed to a small stone placed in the water—barely visible beneath the surface.

"A year ago," he began, "a woman came here, carrying her husband's ashes. She wept as she scattered them into this river. But before she left, she placed this stone just beneath the surface, marking the spot with her silent prayer."

He turned to Padmavathi. "The water has passed over it every day since. New waters. New seasons. The woman has long since passed. But the stone remains. The current touches it still."

He paused.

"Love is like that stone—placed once with deep intent, it endures beneath the flow of life. Bodies return to dust. Words fade from memory. But true love—pure love—settles deeper. It becomes rhythm, resonance. Like a mantra that echoes within the soul long after the sound is gone."

He knelt and dipped his fingers into the flowing river. "Do you feel the water?" he asked.

Padmavathi nodded.

"But you cannot hold it. You cannot keep it," he said. "And yet it touches you. Nourishes you. That is how love lives when the body is gone. Not by being possessed—but by being remembered, felt, absorbed into the very rhythm of our breath."

The villagers stood in silence, watching the ripples where the stone rested beneath the surface—unseen, but present.

The monk then shared a story:

"There once was a flute made of a hollow reed, plain and forgotten. It lay untouched until a dying poet picked it up and played a single note—so full of longing that even the stars wept. The poet passed, but that note echoed through generations. Not because the flute was carved of gold, or the poet was famous, but because the music was real. It came from the soul's edge, from a place beyond language. That one note outlived the lips that breathed it. And became prayer. Presence. Pulse."

Padmavathi stood with closed eyes. A single tear fell—not of sorrow, but of knowing. Her question had not just been answered. It had been heard by the universe.

As the wind stirred through the trees, she whispered almost to herself, "Then perhaps we do not lose them. We become them. We echo their love by how we live."

The monk nodded.

And from that day on, whenever someone in the village asked Padmavathi about her husband, she would smile and say, "I still hear his music… every time I walk by the river."

The sun had begun its descent behind the hills, dyeing the sky in hues of longing—soft amber and aching lavender. The village, wrapped in that mystical hour between day and night, seemed to hold its breath.

Advika, seated with the others beneath the banyan's spreading arms, had been quiet all evening. Her fingers played absently with the hem of her shawl, her gaze lost in the space where the sun had once burned.

Then, as the cicadas began their evening song, she turned toward the monk.

Her voice was steady, yet carried the weight of a question long buried beneath years of strength.

"How do memories of true love continue to shape our present," she asked, "and are we honouring them… or hiding from them?"

There was silence. Not because the question was difficult, but because it was sacred.

Shatananda looked at her—truly looked—as if seeing not just the woman before him, but the echoes she carried. The quiet grief beneath her grace. The love, perhaps, that still lingered like incense in her breath.

They strolled a short distance beyond the banyan grove to an old, quiet house, half-hidden by wild jasmine. Its walls were weathered, but not abandoned. The kind of place where time rested, not passed.

He paused by the gate and said, "This home belonged to Amrit and Leela—two souls deeply bound. They lived here. You wouldn't know them. But they left something behind."

He led her inside. Dust danced in the golden shafts of light streaming through broken shutters. On the mantle lay an old, cracked cup—nothing special. And beside it, a faded painting of a lake at dusk, unfinished.

Shatananda walked to the painting and touched its edge.

"When Leela died suddenly, Amrit stopped painting. He left this one piece incomplete. He would still come here every day, sit by her chair, and whisper the stories they once dreamt together. The village thought he was lost in the past. But one day, I asked him why he returned."

The monk's eyes softened.

"He said, 'Because remembering her makes me more alive, not less. Her love wakes the better parts of me—the parts I'd forget if I tried to move on too fast.'"

He turned to Advika, voice gentler now.

"Memories of true love are not chains. They are roots. And roots don't imprison the tree—they hold it steady in a storm. But when we avoid remembering… when we bury those moments in silence or shame or fear… we let them decay instead of deepen us."

He walked to the old cup.

"This cup," he said, "Leela used it every evening for tea. Amrit never drank from it after she passed—but he polished it every day. Not to preserve the object. But the ritual. The memory. The reverence."

He then spoke more slowly, voice like falling rain on parched soil:

"To honour love is not to speak of it often, but to live in a way that reflects it. When memory shapes our kindness, our courage, our silence—then it is honoured. But when we pretend we were never touched by it—when we hurry to 'move on' or erase the ache—then we hide from it. And from a part of ourselves."

Advika stood in stillness.

She closed her eyes, and in that moment, she saw not the face of the one she had loved and lost, but the mirror of what that love had made her become—more patient, more open, more tender with others.

A tear rolled down her cheek—not for what had ended, but for what had endured.

The monk smiled and said,

"True love never truly leaves. It becomes part of the rhythm of your days—the way you pour water for another, the softness in your voice when no one's watching, the way you hold the silence without fear."

Outside, the jasmine stirred in the twilight breeze.

And that evening, Advika returned to the banyan not with a burden, but with a light—an unseen flame now carried gently in her chest.

CHAPTER IX

Marriage: A Temple of Two Pillars

"Like twin pillars, the strength of love lies not in leaning on each other, but in holding up a shared purpose."

– *Shree Shambav*

The village had never looked so alive.

Children darted through alleyways with marigolds in their hands. Women braided jasmine into long garlands, humming songs passed down like heirlooms. Even the banyan tree, under which Sahasrananda often sat, seemed to shimmer with anticipation.

It was the eve of Anaya and Veer's wedding. But amid the colour and celebration, the couple carried a quiet weight.

They found the monk in the temple courtyard, as the late afternoon sun filtered through ancient stone.

Anaya spoke first, her voice soft but sincere: "Everyone speaks of rituals and promises, but we want to understand... truly—what makes a marriage sacred?"

Sahasrananda looked at them for a long moment—not judging, not instructing, but seeing. Then, without a word, he rose and walked with them toward an old, forgotten corner of the temple.

There stood two weather-worn stone pillars, tall and dignified, their surfaces etched by time.

He gestured to them.

"These two pillars have stood here for centuries. They hold the same temple roof, weather the same monsoons, face the same sun—but they do not lean on one another. See? The space between them allows air to pass, birds to nest, and light to fall."

He paused and continued,

"A sacred marriage is like these pillars. You do not become each other. You do not melt into one. You stand side by side—honouring the space between you. For in that space lies your individual growth, your mystery, your inner sky. Marriage must be closeness without collapse, unity without erasure."

Veer listened, his gaze fixed on the slender cracks in the pillars.

"But what if we drift apart?" he asked quietly.

Sahasrananda smiled gently.

"That is where intention comes in. A temple does not stand because its stones are fused—but because they are placed with precision, with care. So too with love. You must return again and again—not to bind, but to behold."

He then told them a parable:

"'There was once a potter who married a weaver. He shaped clay; she wove silk. At first, they tried to share everything—to blend their crafts. But it only brought tension. One day, they began to sit in silence, side by side. He moulded his pots. She wove her patterns. They didn't speak much—but the rhythm of their hands, the presence of shared air, became their communion. Eventually, his pots bore imprints of silk. And her fabrics took on the curves of vessels. They hadn't merged—but they had mirrored, and in that mirroring, they grew."

He turned to Anaya.

"You may change, and so will he. The question is—can you witness each other's change without fear? Can you evolve together, even as separate souls?"

To Veer, he added,

"Presence is deeper than possession. If you hold a bird too tightly, it suffocates. But if you sit still, it may land on your palm of its own will."

That night, beneath a canopy of stars, the wedding took place.

The priest chanted. The fire danced. But it was in the couple's vows that true meaning stirred:

"I promise to stand beside you—not in shadow, not in dominance, but in shared sun and shared silence. To offer not completion—but companionship. Not to fill your space, but to protect it."

The villagers wept—not from sentimentality, but from recognition. They had seen many weddings, but rarely one that echoed such clarity.

As the music rose and the dancing began, Sahasrananda stepped away quietly. No one noticed. That was how he preferred it.

He walked beneath the stars, humming an old tune, the kind sung not with lips but with the heart.

And behind him, under garlands and candlelight, two pillars now stood—young and human—carrying the sky between them, together.

Marriage is not the union of two halves seeking completion, but the companionship of two whole souls who walk parallel paths. In true love, space is not distance—it is sacred breath. It allows light to pass, individuality to thrive, and the soul to unfold in freedom, while rooted in presence.

As the last notes of the wedding music drifted into silence, children chased fireflies and elders returned to stories. The village, wrapped in soft starlight, felt suspended between celebration and contemplation.

The monk was about to leave when Aadhya, a young girl with curious eyes and a quiet soul, tugged gently at his robe.

She looked up and asked, in a voice that held more wonder than the night sky—

"What is a marriage?"

Sahasrananda looked down, then up again—as if to search the stars for the answer. Instead of speaking, he began to walk. Aadhya followed, her small feet matching his silent steps. The wind rustled through neem leaves above them.

Again, she asked, more softly this time, "What is a marriage?"

And then, like a stream fed by silence and stars, he spoke—not in instruction, but in verse:

Then Aadhya, an inquisitive child, asked—
"What is a marriage?" soft and mild.
The Master walked in silent grace,
A hush of thought upon his face.
She waited, stepping at his side.
Again she asked, eyes open wide:

"What is a marriage?" she implored once more,
The word is like wind upon the shore.
The Master paused, his gaze turned far—
Beyond the hills, beneath a star.
At last he smiled, his voice grew deep,
From wells of silence, thoughts did seep:

"You were born from the same dawn's flame,
And unto the same dusk, you'll return the same.
In life, in death, in soul's pure thread,
You shall be one—though widely spread.
Even where memory meets God's own hush,
Together, you'll rise from dust and crush.

Yet—leave some space in your togetherness,

As moonlight needs the sky's vastness.

Let not your love be clasped too tight—

It breathes, it moves, it seeks the light.

Like breath that lives between two sighs,

Love dances free beneath the skies.

Marriage is music, unseen and fine,

The silence between each sacred line.

Love one another, but don't confine—

Let love be sea, not boundary line.

Flowing from soul to soul untamed,

Not shackled, not owned, not ever named.

Fill one another's cups with grace,

But let your lips find a separate place.

Break bread in joy, yet taste alone—

Each soul must feed from roots its own.

Rejoice, sing, laugh—let spirits soar,

But walk apart on the inner shore.

Like lute strings, tuned yet standing lone,

Together yet each fully grown.

Give all your heart, but do not cage,

For love is not a written page.
It's life itself that holds the key,
Not hands that cling, but souls set free.

Stand close, but not too near to bind,
Like pillars that the roof aligns.
Two trees may share the rain and sun,
Yet grow apart, each reaching one.
Thus, marriage is not a loss of self—
But sacred dance of union and self."

As the night deepened and the wedding lamps flickered in the wind, Surya—Veer's elder brother and a quiet observer—approached the monk. He had watched the ceremony not just with joy, but with the weight of questions unspoken. His own marriage, once vibrant, had become a slow silence.

He sat beside Sahasrananda under the tamarind tree where incense still lingered in the breeze.

With a voice that trembled between introspection and confession, he asked:

"Are we truly honouring our partner as a fellow soul on the path—or are we, perhaps unknowingly, trying to mould them into our reflection?"

The monk did not respond at once. Instead, he picked up the clay lamp placed beside them. The flame danced, flickered, and then steadied.

"Do you see the light?" the monk asked, holding the lamp gently. "This flame burns not because the wick forces the oil to become like it—but because the two meet in balance. The wick holds, the oil nourishes, and the fire rises between them. If either tries to dominate, the flame dies."

He paused, eyes reflecting both moonlight and memory.

"Long ago," he began, "there lived a potter and a painter. The potter shaped clay into bowls with hands weathered by earth. The painter, full of colours and dreams, wished to paint each bowl in his own vision. But every time he tried to force his brush too soon, the clay cracked beneath his touch.

Frustrated, the painter shouted, 'Your vessels are too weak!' The potter replied, 'You see only the surface. You do not wait for them to dry, to breathe. You want them to be what you envision, not what they are.'"

The monk looked at Surya gently, his voice like the hush before rain.

"This is what many do in love. They fall in love with the idea of a person—and then spend years chiselling, shaping, taming. They forget that the soul they met was not theirs to remould, but to witness. To water. To walk beside."

Surya's eyes welled with tears—not of regret, but of recognition. The quiet weight of his own expectations fell before him like petals from an overburdened flower.

Sahasrananda continued:

"To honour your partner is not to see your reflection in them, but to see God's reflection through them. Let them evolve in their own sun and shadow. Let your love be the sky, not the sculptor's chisel. Love them as a fellow traveller, not a project. They are not yours to finish. They are a soul unfolding."

He let the silence sit like a blessing.

Surya whispered, as though to himself, "Maybe love is not about changing another… but changing the way we see them."

The monk smiled, the flame still steady in his hand.

As twilight melted into night, the echoes of wedding chants still hung in the air like the soft trail of incense.

Laughter had slowly quieted. Children had drifted to sleep on their mothers' laps. The fire of the sacred havan pit had reduced to embers, glowing softly in the hush of the village night.

Vaishali, a quiet soul with eyes that always seemed to hold unshed questions, lingered by the edge of the gathering. She was neither old nor young, married nor alone—her path was one of thoughtful solitude. Tonight, something stirred in her heart.

She approached Sahasrananda, who sat watching the moonrise by the riverbank, where fireflies mirrored stars in the dark waters.

She folded her hands and asked gently, "In our closest relationship, do we truly allow space for both togetherness and individuality?"

The monk looked at her for a long time—not with surprise, but with a silence that welcomed her courage. He picked up two small pebbles from the riverbank and held them out.

"What do you see?"

"Two stones," she replied.

"No," he said, "these are companions. They have journeyed down the same stream for years—worn by the same currents, polished by the same tides. But they are not one. They touch, they tumble, they travel close—but they do not merge into a single shape. If they had, they would have lost themselves."

He dropped the stones back into the stream.

Then he turned to her with eyes like dusk meeting dawn.

"Love without space becomes suffocation. And space without love becomes exile. The art of deep companionship lies in knowing when to hold and when to release. When to speak, and when to simply witness."

Vaishali sat beside him, quiet.

He told her a story.

"There once was a woman named Meera and a man named Arjan, married for forty years. Every morning, they would share tea on their veranda. They sat together, yet read different books. One morning, a neighbour asked them, 'Why don't you talk more? Don't you get bored?'

Meera smiled and replied, 'We speak with our presence. We listen to the silence between our words. I don't need Arjan to echo me—I need him to remain who he is, even as he walks beside me.'

When Arjan died years later, Meera still laid out two cups each morning. One for her, one for him. Not in denial—but in devotion. She honoured him not only in their memories of togetherness but in the space he had left untouched—in his chair, in her poems, in the wind that spoke between them."

The monk turned back to the river.

"True closeness," he said, "is like two flutes playing in harmony—not one overpowering the other, but both maintaining their own note. Their music meets in the space between. And it is in that sacred in-between where love breathes, where the soul feels free, and where God listens."

Vaishali looked at the rippling water, her reflection beside his—two faces framed by stars and stillness.

She whispered, "Then, love is not about merging into one shadow—but dancing side by side in the same light."

The monk smiled. "Yes, and in that dance, never forget: the soul longs not to be possessed, but to be seen."

CHAPTER X

The Child Within

"To remember your soul's truth, sometimes you must forget what you've learned and learn how to play again."

– Shree Shambav

The Forgotten Prayer

"In every child's laugh lives a forgotten prayer; in every game, a glimpse of God."

The village square pulsed with a quiet magic. Barefoot feet tapped dust into rhythm, scarves sailed like birds in the breeze, and butterflies danced amid shrieks of laughter. It wasn't just play—it was a kind of sacred music, an orchestra of presence and light.

The monk sat beneath the old neem tree, legs folded, robes soft with earth. He said little. Yet in his stillness, he belonged—like the silence between notes that makes the music whole. He didn't instruct. He simply was. The still point in their spinning world.

A little girl named Meenu, her eyes wide with wonder, tugged gently at his robe and asked, "Why do grown-ups never play?"

The question dropped into the moment like a stone into water, and the ripples lingered. The monk said nothing. Instead, he bent, picked up a flat stone, and with a flick of his fingers, sent it skimming into their circle. The children cheered.

He had entered their world—not as a teacher, but as one of them.

The game resumed—stones, riddles, laughter. The monk offered no corrections, gave no commands. He followed, he listened. And in that listening, he taught.

The Scoff of the World

An elder passed by, arms crossed, eyes furrowed with pride and age. With a scoff just loud enough to sting, he muttered, "He wastes time with children."

But the village square had become more than a place of barter and business. It had become a temple—where the sacred wore no robes, but ran barefoot and laughed wildly. What once echoed with trade now rang with joy—pure, unfiltered, rising like incense to the open sky.

The monk often sat by the well, eyes soft with memory. He did not teach the children—he played with them. He laughed when they laughed, listened when they spoke in dreams. His silence wasn't absence; it was presence, deep and undivided.

One afternoon, rain began to fall. The children danced, arms wide, faces turned to the sky. Elders frowned, but the monk smiled.

"Let them dance," he said softly. "This rain doesn't just fall on their skin—it baptises their spirit."

An old farmer grunted, "What of wisdom? What of dignity?"

The monk replied, "Wisdom isn't always solemn. Sometimes, it skips barefoot through puddles. Dignity isn't in seriousness—it's in sincerity. And a child's joy... that is the sincerest prayer the world has forgotten how to say."

Then, almost to himself, he whispered,

"If only we remembered—not just who we became, but who we were before the world taught us to forget."

In the embrace of gratitude, content with what I hold,

Not yearning for what's absent, a heart's desire untold,

Less concerned with appearances, judgments I'd dismiss,

Oh, to return to childhood's realm of eternal bliss.

Opinions of others do matter not, my thoughts take flight,

Seriousness abandoned, replaced by joy and delight,

Playfulness reigns supreme, with laughter as my guide,

Oh, to reclaim the innocence lost, to be a child inside.

With less knowledge of others, my focus turned within,

Selflessness over self-concern, newfound kin,

To care and understand, ignorance's bliss I'd embrace,

Oh, to relive the purity of childhood's grace.

Dancing in pure elation, worries cast away,

Finding beauty in shadows, in rainbows that sway,

A carefree existence, untouched by sorrow's reign,

Oh, to rediscover life's essence, free from adult strain.

Running through fields, marvelling at avian flight,

Chasing darkness, mesmerised by stars' celestial light,

Unfazed by external stains, my soul's purity intact,

Oh, to revisit innocence, without blemish, in fact.

Trust bestowed upon friends, betrayal's fear erased,

Basking in the sun's warmth, its radiance embraced,

Dancing in rain's embrace, unbothered by being wet,

Oh, to relish in childlike trust, without regret.

Innocence devoid of falsehood, love for all unbound,

Smiling at every being, humility profound,

Hugs replacing tugs, compassion leading the way,

Oh, to recapture that pure love as a child each day.

Living life fully unburdened by time's hold,

Past, present, and future merging, stories yet untold,

Wonder is found in the smallest; life's miracles unfold,

Oh, to embody the child's awe, forever young, bold.

Oh, if I were a child again, my heart yearns to be,

Embracing life's wonders, forever wild and free,

To see the world through innocent eyes, pure and unfeigned,

Oh, if I were a child again, a timeless wish ingrained.

A Story Within the Silence

A boy curled up in his lap. The monk looked up at the villagers and said, "They remember what we've forgotten."

Then came the hush—that quiet before the first monsoon drop—and he spoke:

"There once was a king, wise and powerful, ruler of lands vast and rich. But peace never touched his palace. Philosophers debated in his halls, dancers spun in golden light, yet his heart was heavy.

In old age, a grandchild was born. One morning, he heard the child giggling—rolling a mango across marble. He paused. Something stirred.

Days passed. The child crawled into his arms, hid behind the curtains, and squealed with delight. The court whispered: 'Has he lost his dignity?'

But the king? He had finally found joy.

He told his ministers, 'I governed kingdoms with law—but only a child's laughter governed my soul. I had to grow old to become young again.'"

The Village Remembers

The monk looked out at them—shoemakers, potters, weavers—and said,

"Watch the children. Don't rush to teach. Just watch. Their wonder is not ignorance—it is remembrance. They are closer to the Source than we are. Their laughter is a mantra. Their awe is prayer. They do not seek meaning. They live it."

And slowly, something began to shift.

The cobbler laid down his tools and chased a fluttering leaf with his son. The potter began spinning not just clay, but stories with his daughter. Mothers sang lullabies not to hush, but to invite dancing.

The village was not learning anything new.

It was remembering something sacred.

Ramesh asked, "When did you last see the world through a child's eyes—without judgment, fear, or pride?"

The question settled into the silence like dew on morning grass—gentle, glistening, and awakening something forgotten. The circle around the monk grew still. Even the wind seemed to pause, waiting not for an answer, but for remembrance.

The monk, seated beside the village well, opened his eyes slowly. He looked not at Ramesh but at the sky, where a lone bird cut across the golden dusk. Then he spoke—not immediately with words, but with a softness that wrapped around the space like a shawl.

"There was once a sculptor," the monk began, his voice barely above the breeze, "who carved angels from stone. With each passing year, his work grew more flawless—perfect symmetry, polished wings, majestic expressions. Kings bought his art, and poets sang of his chisels. But he felt... hollow. The statues were admired, yet they no longer sang to him as they once did when he was young.

One day, he visited the village where he was born. There, in a corner of the old temple courtyard, he found one of his earliest works—forgotten by the world, weathered by rain and time. It was rough, uneven, the wings crooked, the face incomplete. But it had something the others did not—a spark. A kind of innocence that reached into his chest and stirred something buried deep.

He wept. Not because the sculpture was beautiful, but because he had forgotten how to see. He had once carved not to impress, but to express. Not too perfect, but to play.

He sat beside that statue for hours, tracing the imperfections with his hands. And in that moment, he realised—it wasn't technique he had lost. It was the eyes through which he once beheld the world."

The monk turned gently to Ramesh, his voice now rich with feeling.

"To see through a child's eyes is not to be blind—it is to see without the dust of judgment, the armour of pride, or the shadows of fear. It is to see the world not as a battlefield, but as a playground of mystery. To watch a raindrop chase another on a window and call it a race. To hold a fallen leaf and believe it flew. To meet someone and ask not their status, but, 'Will you play with me?'"

He paused, as if tasting the air for memory.

"A child does not walk through a forest naming species or calculating yield. He walks in awe, whispering to the trees, believing they whisper back.

And maybe they do—but only to those who have not yet forgotten how to listen."

He lifted a small pebble and tossed it gently into the nearby pond.

"This is our vision," he said, watching the ripples. "When we are young, the water is clear. Every leaf, cloud, and moonbeam reflects with wonder. Then, over time, the waters are stirred by ambition, comparison, wounds, and worry. We stop seeing the sky reflected. We see only the surface disturbances."

Then, looking back at Ramesh, he added,

"But the sky never left. Nor was the clarity. Only the stillness did. And stillness... can return."

The Invitation

"Go," the monk said at last, smiling gently. "Find a tree and sit beneath it. Watch the clouds until they stop being data. Let the wind touch you without needing a reason. Chase a butterfly—not to catch it, but to remember that once, you too had wings.

And when you meet your reflection again, you may just find the child still waiting—eyes wide, hands open, heart unafraid."

That was Ramesh's answer. Not in explanation—but in awakening.

Some questions are not meant to be answered with thoughts.

They are meant to be lived—until the child within you stops waiting... and starts playing again.

Vasudevan asked, "What lessons have you ignored from those younger than you?"

The question, spoken quietly, carried the weight of unseen mirrors. It did not accuse—it revealed. The monk remained motionless, but the smile that slowly spread across his face was not amusement. It was remembrance.

He looked at Vasudevan—not as a teacher to a student, but as a fellow traveller.

"There is a story I once heard," the monk began, his voice like a gentle breeze through old leaves, "about a sage who spent forty years mastering scriptures, meditating in caves, and walking barefoot across kingdoms. He was revered far and wide, called the living flame of wisdom.

One day, a child wandered into his hermitage—muddy, curious, and laughing at birds. The sage, trying to meditate, asked him to sit still.

The boy giggled and said, 'Why? The birds are not still. The wind isn't still. Why must I be?'

The sage scolded gently, 'Stillness brings you closer to the Divine.'

The child replied, 'But isn't the Divine also playing? Why else would butterflies exist?'"

The monk paused and let the silence deepen before continuing:

"The sage, for the first time in years, couldn't answer. That night, he sat not in lotus posture, but with his knees tucked to his chest, watching the stars. He remembered the days when he too had laughed without reason, when a puddle was an ocean, and a firefly was a lantern from heaven. And he wept—not because the boy had made him feel small, but because he had grown too tall to see what the boy still could."

The monk turned to Vasudevan and said softly:

"We think wisdom flows downward, from old to young, as rivers to the sea. But what if it also rises—like sap from a seed, like laughter from a child's heart?"

He touched the earth beside him.

"Children come into the world carrying truths we spend lifetimes unlearning. They forgive easily, feel fully, ask without shame, and wonder without need for reason. And we... call them naïve."

He looked around the circle.

"But who is truly naïve? The one who sees magic in the moon, or the one who sees only rock and dust? The one who dances in the rain, or the one who rushes for cover?"

Monk continued, "There was a boy in the village once—Raju. Poor, barefoot, always smiling. He offered me a guava one morning and said, 'It's not from my tree, but the tree doesn't mind.' I asked him how he knew.

He replied, 'Because it never asks me to say thank you.'

That day, I realised: He knew more about unconditional giving than I did—even after years of teaching about compassion."

"A young tree bends with the wind; an old one may crack. The young are like flowing water—fresh, spontaneous, unshaped by walls. But we build dams around them, trying to 'civilise' their wildness, not realising that in doing so, we often dam the Divine.

Their questions are not always meant to be answered—they are mirrors to our forgotten selves. Their joy is not chaos—it is remembrance."

The Invitation

He looked back at Vasudevan and said with warmth:

"So ask yourself: When did a younger soul try to teach you something you dismissed? A lesson in patience? In honesty? In awe?

Maybe it was a child who refused to be bribed by praise. Or a teenager who told the truth you were afraid to say. Or a young heart that showed you how to love without needing a reason."

The monk smiled gently, as if peering into memory itself. His eyes weren't fixed on anyone, but seemed to look inward—toward a place time had not touched. The question still lingered in the air: What lessons have you ignored from those younger than you?

Instead of replying directly, he let the silence breathe for a while. Then, in a voice that felt like rain returning to thirsty soil, he spoke—not in explanation, but in verse.

There lives a young one in me who will not die,

A flicker of the past I cannot deny.

He's no longer me, yet we still entwine—

His eyes meet mine through the mirror's shine.

He searches the glass for a truth unclear,

For laughter lost, for dreams held dear.

"Where is the dance? The song? The flame?

Did you live well, or forget my name?"

I chase his gaze, that shimmering thread,
A voice within that I thought was dead.
His questions echo like midnight rain—
Soft drops of memory, touched by pain.
"You once believed the world was kind,
But traded joy for an anxious mind.
Your dreams," he sighs, "were light and frail,
And truth, too heavy for hope to sail."

I have become what I am today—
The path I walked, the price I pay.
All I chased, all I earned and knew—
Is this what the child in me once drew?
The man I am, the one I became—
Is he the torchbearer, or just the flame?
Am I the dream, or the one who woke?
Or both—entwined in a fragile yoke?

What stole the sparkle from my gaze,
The wonder once found in simpler days?
Was it the race, the climb, the prize,
That dimmed the stars in youthful skies?

No more the chase for butterflies,
Nor songs beneath the open skies.
No barefoot dance beneath the rain,
Just silent walks through glass and grain.

I once sang like the koel at dawn,
Loved without names, no roles to don.
Played under trees with muddy feet,
Moonlit fields, where fireflies meet.
Watched frogs croak in monsoon glee,
Felt the world as it played with me.
Was that innocence, or was it grace—
To live in time, not run the race?

Why now do I feel so far removed,
From all the things that once had soothed?
Why can't I be who I once knew—
The soul untouched, the self so true?
I wear the years like borrowed skin,
Yet hear the child still call within.
There lives a young one who will not die—
A whisper beneath my grown-up cry.

He stares from mirrors, asks no more,

Just lingers behind memory's door.

He longs not to rule, nor rise, nor win—

Just to feel the rain upon his skin.

And until the day I stop the lie

That I outgrew him, said goodbye—

He lives in me, a silent hymn,

A timeless echo—I am still him.

As the final lines of the poem faded like dusk over the mountains, a stillness settled over the gathering. No one dared to speak, as if even their breath might disturb the quiet grace that had entered the space.

The monk looked up, his voice softer now, but clear:

"Youth may not have the map. But sometimes, they still remember the direction."

And in that still moment under the banyan tree, it was no longer clear who was the elder, and who the student. The faces, young and old, seemed to blur—like reflections on a rippling pond.

Wisdom had stopped flowing in one direction.

It had become a circle.

CHAPTER XI

Live Like a Flower

"A flower never asks for permanence, yet its fragrance lingers in every heart it touches."

– *Shree Shambav*

The sun was soft that morning—neither shy nor bold—just warm enough to stir the scent of earth and awaken the sleepy dew resting on the garden leaves. In the corner where the marigolds bloomed, little Aashi sat cross-legged, her fingers carefully cupping a golden blossom as though it were made of sunlight. Her eyes sparkled with the innocent awe of someone who had just discovered a miracle.

Each morning, she greeted that flower. She whispered to it, sang lullabies from forgotten rhymes, and told it secrets only a child's heart could carry. And in return, the marigold seemed to bloom just for her—radiant, wild, alive.

But that day, something had changed.

The petals drooped, their fire extinguished. The stem leaned tiredly, its once-proud posture surrendered to the soil. Aashi's breath caught. She reached out with trembling fingers, touching what had once danced in the breeze. Tears welled in her eyes—hot, confused tears that carried a question deeper than her years could explain.

"Why did it have to die?" she whispered, not knowing if she was asking the sky, the earth, or her own aching heart.

Sahasrananda, the monk who tended the monastery's gardens, had been watching from a distance. He walked slowly toward her, his robes trailing like river currents behind him. His eyes were not filled with answers, but with presence. He knelt beside her.

Taking the withered flower gently into his weathered palm, he studied it for a moment—as if it were not dead, but resting from a dance only few understood.

Then, in a voice softer than falling rain, he said, "Because it lived so fully, little one, it had no fear of death."

Aashi looked up at him, puzzled. Her grief made her quiet, but her heart was still listening.

He continued, "In a sacred valley, far beyond these mountains, the flowers bloom for just a single day.

Only one. At sunrise, they unfold in joy. They know their time is short. But they do not weep. They bloom with all their colours, spread their fragrance into the air, and offer their beauty to the world without holding anything back. They live so completely that by sunset, they bow to the earth—not in sorrow, but in fulfilment."

He placed the marigold gently on the soil, as one might return a sacred offering to the altar of life.

"The marigold did not fail you, Aashi," he said, brushing her cheek with a tenderness only years of silence could teach. "It completed its journey. And now, it returns—not to end, but to begin again."

He handed her a small cloth pouch filled with seeds—the promise hidden inside loss.

"Scatter these," he said, "Let the wind carry them. Beauty is not meant to stay. It's meant to return."

Aashi stood quietly, her small hands grasping the seeds as if holding tiny stars. She opened her palm and let them fly. The breeze caught them gently, lifting them like wishes into the waiting sky.

A smile returned to her face—not the same one as before. This one had a tear in it, a knowing, a depth. The first smile of someone who has glimpsed the mystery beneath the veil.

She turned to the monk, her eyes wide with a question that was as much prayer as it was wonder.

"Can I bloom too," she asked, "even if I fade one day?"

The monk's smile deepened like the roots of an old tree. He placed his hand over his heart and nodded.

A flower's beauty can move us to tears,

With its soft petals and vibrant colours, so dear,

It blooms in quietness, a symbol of grace,

Bringing joy and hope to any space.

As it sways in the gentle breeze,

We can't help but feel at ease,

Watching it dance in pure delight,

A wonder to behold, a true delight.

Flowers may seem fragile, but don't be deceived,

For they're resilient and won't be aggrieved,

By strong winds or heavy rains,

They'll stand tall and weather the pains.

Their fragility belies a fierce will to live,

And they remind us to cherish and give,

To nurture and care for all that's alive,

To embrace the fleeting moments and thrive.

So, next time you see a flower, by the way,

Pause and listen to what it has to say.

For it may whisper a message of love,

Or offer a reminder from above.

Live your life like a flower: pure and bright,

Dancing with joy during the day and night,

Leaving a trail of beauty and memories,

For others to cherish, to hold, and to seize.

"Especially then," he said. "It is not how long you bloom that matters—it's how fully. To bloom even while knowing you'll fade... that is grace."

A silence fell between them, the kind that makes the soul feel held. In that hush, the garden seemed to breathe. The sun warmed the Earth. The seeds drifted, unseen, into new soil.

And Aashi, though still a child, walked away a little more like a flower—open, soft, and brave enough to live fully, even if only for a little while.

Under the golden canopy of a quiet afternoon, Sarika's voice broke the silence like a soft chime in the wind. Her question was not casual—it came from a place inside her that had tasted love and loss, beauty and impermanence. She looked not at the monk, but at a marigold petal crumbling in her palm, as if asking the fading flower itself.

"Can you find beauty even in what fades—and love it without needing to keep it?"

Sahasrananda did not answer immediately. He watched her fingers tremble slightly, as if reluctant to release even the withered petal. The earth held many secrets, but few as delicate as this: the art of holding and letting go at once.

He drew a slow breath and said, "Once, in a land far from here, there was a woman who embroidered tapestries so beautiful that kings and mystics came to gaze upon them. But she had a strange custom—once a piece was complete, she would burn it. She believed that beauty was not meant to be preserved like a fossil, but lived like a breath—deep, full, and free."

Sarika's brows furrowed. "But why destroy something so beautiful?"

The monk smiled gently, his eyes resting on the falling sunlight flickering through the banyan leaves. "Because even beauty, when caged, forgets how to breathe. And even love, when gripped too tightly, begins to ache under the weight of possession."

He picked up a dry leaf and twirled it in his fingers. "What fades teaches us the truth of presence. A flower that blooms for a single day gives more fragrance than one that fears the night. A sunset that slips away teaches the eye to see more fiercely. The heart breaks not because beauty ends—but because we believe it should have lasted forever."

Sarika was quiet. A breeze passed through her hair like a whisper from something older than memory.

"Have you ever watched a bird," he asked, "and felt joy in its flight—knowing it will not stay? Can you love like that? Can you see beauty as a flame—meant not to be held, but felt in its warmth, even as it vanishes?"

Sarika finally opened her palm and let the marigold petal fall to the earth. It drifted down like a tiny sun returning to the soil.

"I think," she said softly, "I'm beginning to understand. That some things become more beautiful because they end."

The monk touched her shoulder lightly. "That is the doorway to sacred love—to love without clinging, to see with reverence what is fleeting. When you do that, you are no longer just loving beauty. You are becoming it."

And in that moment, Sarika wasn't just a girl asking a question. She became the question itself—open, raw, and quietly radiant.

Like the flower that knows it will wither by dusk, and yet opens fully at dawn… She, too, began to bloom.

Ananya sat beside the monk near the temple garden. A gentle breeze rustled the marigolds, their orange heads nodding like elders whispering ancient truths. She held a half-bloomed bud between her fingers, its petals just beginning to unfurl, trembling as if unsure whether to open or stay hidden. Her voice came quietly, almost like a thought spoken aloud:

"What part of our life, like a flower, needs to be lived fully before it withers?"

Sahasrananda didn't reply at once. Instead, he turned his gaze toward the distant mountains, lost in a silence that held more than absence of words—it held memory. Then, slowly, he began to speak, not with haste, but with reverence, as one does when brushing dust from something sacred.

"There was once a young prince," he said, "who was told by an oracle that he would die before his hair turned grey. Fearful of death, he locked himself away—no journeys, no love, no risks. He lived long but hollow. And when his end came, the gods wept—not because he died early, but because he had never truly lived."

Ananya's eyes darkened with thought, her fingers loosening their hold on the bud.

"Life is not measured only by years," the monk continued, "but by intensity, sincerity, and presence. Some parts of us—like youth, wonder, trust, or a chance at love—have their season. They are like wildflowers: if you wait too long, they'll be gone with the next wind. Not because they were cruel, but because they were gifts for a moment."

He paused and then leaned slightly closer. "Tell me, Ananya, have you ever danced in the rain without wondering if someone is watching? Have you said 'I love you' while your heart still beat wildly with truth—not after it calcified into caution? Have you embraced your curiosity before fear taught it silence?"

Her lips parted, then closed. Her eyes welled not with sorrow, but recognition.

He pointed to a nearby marigold, fully open, glowing in the sun. "That flower didn't wait for permission to bloom. It opened because that was its purpose, even if it only had a day. What in you is waiting for permission?"

She looked down, tears slipping quietly down her cheeks—not of regret, but of awakening.

"My voice," she whispered. "My song. I've silenced it for fear of being unheard."

Sahasrananda placed a hand over his heart. "Then sing, child. Not because the world must listen—but because the song is yours. That part of you, like the flower, must be lived fully before it fades. Let it bloom, even if no one claps. Let it bloom because it is meant to."

Ananya stood, still crying, but with a strange smile blooming across her face. She walked into the garden and stood amidst the flowers, lifting her face to the sky as if ready to sing her forgotten song—not later, not when the time was perfect, but now.

And in that moment, even the flowers seemed to pause and listen. Because a heart that chooses to bloom before withering... Becomes a garden the world will never forgets.

CHAPTER XII

Ashes and the Lamp

"Some fires do not come to destroy us, but to awaken the wings we forgot we had."

– Shree Shambav

The Fire That Took

It began as a flicker on the horizon, barely noticeable in the golden hush of late afternoon. But winds have no master, and flames have no conscience.

By the time the villagers saw the smoke rising from the edge of their fields, it was too late. Fire does not ask for permission. It took with it grain that had been blessed by calloused hands, homes that had been mended with generations of care, and dreams sown into the soil with silent prayers.

People stood stunned—some wept openly, others cursed the gods, others simply collapsed to their knees in disbelief. The smoke wasn't just in the sky—it was inside their hearts. What do you do when everything you've built is taken in a single afternoon?

The Monk Walks In

He did not run. He did not cry out. He did not chant mantras to plead with the heavens.

Sahasrananda walked into the village like a still breeze before a storm. He carried no words—only presence.

He did not offer the usual comfort of a teacher. No scriptures were quoted. No cosmic justifications were made. He walked with dust on his robes and ash in his hair, as if the grief of the people had passed through him like the fire itself.

He walked to the centre of the broken village where a farmer sat on the ground, his head in his hands, sobbing not just for his house, but for the years it took to build it.

Sahasrananda knelt beside him.

Then, wordlessly, he began to clear the debris with his bare hands.

The Rhythm of Hands

One by one, others followed.

A young boy brought a bucket. An old woman picked up charred wood. A mother, still wiping her tears, began clearing the ashes from the schoolroom floor.

No one spoke. Yet the silence was alive. It had rhythm, like breath. Like mourning made into motion.

It wasn't about fixing anything in that moment. It was about belonging to the pain—together. It was the sacred act of witnessing one another's wounds and deciding not to turn away.

The monk's silence was not indifference. It was a silent prayer offered through action: I am with you—not above you. Let my hands do the praying.

The Lamp and the Phoenix

That night, under a sky that had finally cleared, the people gathered.

They didn't know why, but something in them longed for his presence again—not for answers, but for meaning.

Sahasrananda lit a single oil lamp and placed it on a rock. The flame flickered gently, like a new heartbeat.

He looked at them for a long moment. Then, softly, he spoke.

"There is a bird in the ancient forests far to the east. It lives for a hundred years in beauty and peace. When its time comes, it does not run from the fire—it sings to it. It builds its own pyre and wraps itself in flames.

And from the ashes, it is born again—its feathers brighter, its flight even stronger. Not in spite of the fire, but because of it.

That bird is called the Phoenix."

He paused and let the silence fill the night once more.

"Pain will visit, like fire. It may burn down what we thought would last forever. But if we hold each other through the flame, something new can rise—not the same as before, but truer. Braver. Kinder."

The road of life is winding, with twists and turns ahead,

With hills to climb and valleys that must be tread.

And in the journey, we'll face tough times and strife,

That will test our spirit, and challenge our life.

But tough times are not meant to break us or defeat,

But to shape us, to mould us, and make us complete.

For in the furnace of adversity, we're forged like steel,

Stronger and braver, with a heart that can heal.

And though the journey may be long, and the path unclear,
We remember these struggles are meant to adhere.
For we are warriors, with hearts that are brave and true,
And we have the strength to persevere and make it through.

These hardships are the forge that tempers the soul,
The crucible is where we grow and learn to be whole.
Where we find resilience when all seems lost and undone,
And rise again to fight and to overcome.

So, when life gets tough, and the winds do blow,
Remember that you have what it takes to glow.
Tough times in life are not meant to define,
But to refine and strengthen, so you can shine.

The Night After

There was no applause. No grand realisation.

Just a village lying down in quiet acceptance, soot still in their hair, hearts still cracked—but no longer alone.

They had not avoided the fire. They had walked through it. Together.

Sahasrananda remained awake, watching the lamp flicker. He spoke to no one. But in his stillness, something sacred was shared: The fire takes—but it also reveals the gold beneath.

The Healing Power of Presence

Saraswathi's question came not as curiosity, but as a tremor from her own memory. Her voice, though steady, held the ache of something lived. "When pain arrives like an unexpected storm, how can silence and presence offer more healing than answers?"

He began, not with an explanation, but a story.

The Boy and the Rain

Years ago, in a village far north, a boy lost his mother during childbirth. He was five—too young to understand death, yet old enough to feel the sudden stillness of her absence. The days after her passing were filled with people: relatives came, priests chanted, neighbours spoke in hushed tones and offered platitudes.

But none of it touched the boy.

Not because he didn't hear them, but because their words floated like dry leaves across a stormy sea.

"She's in a better place," they said. "Time will heal," they offered. But what does a child know of time?

Then, late one evening, as the last guest left and the boy sat alone in a corner clutching his mother's scarf, his grandfather walked in.

He said nothing.

He sat beside the boy on the mud floor, pulled him gently into his arms, and together they watched the rain fall for hours. No words. Just the rhythm of rain, and the quiet of being together.

It was not an answer. It was a presence.

And in that presence, the boy felt the first thread of healing—a silent thread woven not through explanation, but through shared stillness.

Sahasrananda turned to the gathered villagers and continued:

"When a storm strikes, do we shout at the wind to stop? Do we stand beneath the thunder and argue with the lightning? No. We shelter the flame. We hold one another close. We wait.

Words are like fire in a storm—they often scatter, unable to root. But presence… presence is like a warm blanket around the soul. It says, without saying: 'You're not alone. I will not run from your pain.'"

The Wisdom of the Silent Tree

The monk pointed to the ancient neem tree that had withstood decades of storms.

"Look at that tree. It does not lecture the wind. It bends. It listens. It holds the soil. And after the storm passes, the tree is still there—quietly offering shade, roots deepened by what it endured."

In the same way, silence can become sacred—not the absence of care, but the highest form of compassion. It does not try to fix, because it understands that pain is not a problem to be solved, but a sacred space to be held.

A Moment in the Village

Saraswathi, who had asked the question, looked down at her hands. She remembered the day she lost her child—how everyone had tried to console her with words that felt like thorns wrapped in silk. But the one thing she remembered most was not what anyone said… it was the moment her sister sat beside her, silently weeping, and held her hand all night.

No words. Just presence.

A wound shared, not explained.

A silence that did not avoid the pain—but honoured it.

"Answers live in the mind," the monk said, "but healing begins in the heart. And the heart speaks a language older than words—one of touch, breath, nearness.

When we sit beside someone in pain without the need to explain it away, we become the shelter. We become the tree. We become the balm that words could never be."

And in that quiet, Saraswathi closed her eyes—not to avoid the world, but to finally feel it. She wasn't seeking answers anymore.

She had found something better.

A companion in the storm.

From the Ashes, We Rise: The Sacred Art of Rebuilding Together

Apoorva stepped forward slowly, the glow of firelight still flickering in her eyes from the recent blaze. Her voice carried the gravity of grief, but also the quiet strength of one who had not turned away from pain.

She asked, "What can we rebuild together in the ashes of what was lost?"

Sahasrananda listened in stillness.

The fire had devoured homes, fields, memories—yes. But it had also uncovered something that had long gone unseen. Not in the earth, but in the hearts of the people.

He began to speak—not with instructions, but with a memory.

The Story of the Broken Temple

Years ago, in a small Himalayan hamlet, there stood a temple built entirely of cedarwood—no nails, only interlocking beams, carved by ancestors with reverent hands. It was more than a place of worship; it was the village's soul.

One winter, a freak lightning storm struck. The temple caught fire and crumbled into ash. The villagers, shattered, stood for days around its ruins, paralysed by the weight of loss.

Everyone waited for the head priest to speak. But he said nothing. Instead, he knelt down and began to pick up charred fragments—one by one—and placed them in a circle. People were confused. It was just blackened wood, some barely recognisable.

But slowly, as the days passed, others joined. Someone brought a broken bell. Another brought melted brass figurines. An old woman came with incense and a handful of temple dust wrapped in cloth. They began to place these fragments together—not to rebuild the temple as it was, but to create a sacred space from what remained.

No grand blueprint. No old hierarchy.

Just presence. Effort. Intention.

Weeks passed.

The new space that emerged was unlike the temple before—it had no walls, no roof, only a central altar made of blackened cedar and wildflowers. Yet people came. Prayers returned. And something deeper rose—not in stone or wood, but in unity.

The village didn't rebuild a temple.

They rebuilt themselves.

Kintsugi and the Human Soul

"What can we rebuild together?" the monk echoed. "Everything that matters."

When something breaks in Japan, the art of Kintsugi teaches that we do not discard it. We mend the cracks with gold, making the broken places more visible—more beautiful. The object becomes not less valuable, but more meaningful because of its fractures.

And isn't that what community is?

Not the absence of scars—but the decision to weave them into something sacred. Together.

"Loss burns away the false walls we build around ourselves," he said. "And in the ashes, we find each other. Real. Raw. Ready."

Monk, after a pause said:

"We rebuild not by restoring what was, but by giving new meaning to what remains. In the ashes, there is memory—but also seeds.

In our shared sorrow, we rediscover strength not in solitude, but in we.

It is not about building back the same walls. It is about becoming a sanctuary for one another."

That evening, as the stars watched quietly, Apoorva walked to the edge of the fields—still blackened by flame—and knelt down. Not in defeat. But with her hands in the soil.

A place had been lost.

But a people had been found.

And in that truth, they began again.

PART THREE

The House the Soul Built

"Power is not a throne one sits upon, but a storm one learns to stand within. The moment you believe you control it, it begins to control you."

- *Shree Shambav*

CHAPTER XIII

Home: More Than Shelter

"A house made of stone protects the body—but only love, silence, and presence can build a home for the soul."

– Shree Shambav

The sun had just begun to soften, casting long golden threads across the Monk's Garden. Children ran, their laughter chasing butterflies through marigold beds, while elders quietly tended the soil with reverence and rhythm. The monk, silent and serene, moved among them with a watering pot in hand—pausing now and then to whisper to the plants, as if nourishing more than just roots.

Aadhya, curious as ever, stopped her game of tag and wandered toward him. Her voice, clear and unburdened by the complexities of adulthood, cut through the breeze.

"What is a house?" she asked, brushing her fingers against a flower.

The monk paused mid-pour. A drop of water hung on the lip of the can, trembling like an unshed tear. He looked at her—not with the urgency to explain, but with the softness of someone about to offer a sacred memory.

He placed the pot down beside the tulsi plant, stood up slowly, and began to speak—not as a teacher, but as someone remembering.

"There once lived a wealthy merchant," he said, "who built a house as grand as his name. Tall marble pillars, silk curtains from foreign lands, chandeliers that mimicked stars—each corner whispered of gold, but not of warmth. He had everything… except rest."

The monk's voice flowed gently, like water running over smooth stones. The children had begun to gather now, quieting, drawn to the hush in his tone.

"One monsoon night, a storm came—not of rain alone, but of fate. The winds howled like ancient spirits reclaiming what was never truly his. In the morning, there were no walls left. Just rubble. Just silence."

He looked into the distance as if watching the memory unfold before his eyes.

"With nowhere to go, he found shelter in the home of a poor farmer's family. Their house was small—mud walls, a leaky roof, a single lamp. But there was laughter at dinner, prayers at dawn, and warmth in every gesture. The children played barefoot. The parents shared their last roti without hesitation. There were no chandeliers... but there was light."

He bent to pull a weed from a flowerbed, his touch gentle.

"Days turned into weeks. And the merchant, once proud and alone, began helping them build a new room. Brick by brick, something changed in him. He realised: his old house had protected his body, but never cradled his soul. It echoed with emptiness even when filled with guests."

The monk turned toward the children now, his eyes glistening not with sorrow, but understanding.

"So when he built again—he built differently. Not just with stone, but with story. Not just with locks, but with listening. He learned that a house is not just a place you live in—it is a space that breathes with you. A house becomes a home when it holds your silence without judgment, your laughter without envy, and your tears without shame."

The wind rustled through the garden as if bowing in agreement.

"Walls are for protection. But what shelters us in truth is presence. What makes us feel at home is love—quiet, ordinary, sacred love."

The children were silent now. Not because they understood every word—but because they felt them.

Aadhya whispered, "So... home is where the heart feels safe?"

The monk smiled, eyes twinkling.

"Yes, little one. And sometimes, we have to lose what we built with our hands to discover what we can build with heart."

He lifted the watering pot again, and with a final glance at the blooming jasmine, added softly,

"A house shelters the body. But a home… a true home... is where your soul can exhale."

Monk, after a pause, recited the verse:

A storm once stole his roof and wall,

Left marble halls to dust and fall.

He chased in gold what couldn't stay—

And watched it vanish in a day.

A hut of clay with laughter lit,

Where strangers let his sorrow sit.

No silk, no crown, no chandelier—

Just warmth that drew his spirit near.

He watched their hands make bread and song,

Their silence deep, their roots grown strong.

Each word a flame, each smile a thread—

A home where even grief was fed.

He laid new bricks with humbled hands,

No longer lost in life's demands.

And as the walls rose from the dust,

He built on love—not wealth or trust.

Now hearths may fade, and stones depart,

But not the house built in the heart.

A place where spirit finds its flame—

Where walls dissolve, and none need name.

As the wind rustled through the peepal leaves above them. Aadhya looked at the monk watering a small tulsi plant. Her brow was furrowed in curiosity.

Aadhya nodded thoughtfully, then tilted her head. "What is clothing, Guruji? Why do we all dress differently?"

The monk paused, setting the pot gently beside the roots. His eyes softened as if he were looking beyond the moment, into another time.

He said, "Let me tell you a story, child—not of kings or gods, but of a tailor and a prince."

The Story of the Naked Prince and the Invisible Thread

Once, in a distant kingdom, there lived a prince who had never worn common clothes. Silks from Persia, jewels from across the seas—his garments were stitched with pride, not thread. He believed his identity lay in the richness he wore. People bowed to him, not because of who he was, but what shimmered on his skin.

One day, while journeying through a forest, the prince was caught in a storm. His guards fled, his carriage overturned, and his robes were torn by thorn and rain. Cold and frightened, he stumbled into a humble village.

A poor tailor took him in. The prince asked for his royal cloak, but the tailor simply handed him a clean, coarse robe and said, "First, wear comfort before status. Here, no one greets the cloth before the man."

The prince stayed there, ashamed at first—until he saw that everyone, old and young, wore simple clothes but carried themselves with quiet dignity. Their clothes weren't loud, yet their hearts spoke volumes.

One evening, the tailor showed him a tattered tunic stitched with dozens of odd fabrics. "This," he said, "was made from the pieces people gave me—my mother's sari, my son's shawl, a stranger's gift when I had nothing. Each stitch holds a story, a relationship, a lesson."

The prince was silent. For the first time, he realised his silk had never told a story—it had only hidden his silence.

Years later, even after returning to his palace, the prince chose to wear simple robes. His court mocked him at first, but soon, the people began to see him, not just the garments. His words carried more weight, because they came not from a costumed figure—but from a soul clothed in humility.

The Monk Turned to Aadhya

He said gently, "Clothes are not wrong, dear one. They protect us, honour occasions, and express culture and emotion. But when they become masks—when they separate rather than connect—they turn from fabric to fiction."

"We dress differently because we are diverse in soul and story. But when we begin to believe that what we wear is who we are—we forget the invisible clothing that matters most: kindness, dignity, honesty, love."

He smiled, brushing a petal off Aadhya's shoulder.

"Your true clothing, my child, is the way your presence touches another soul. That, no needle can stitch, and no moth can eat."

We dress in thread, in silk and pride,

To show the world what dwells inside.

Yet oft the cloth becomes disguise,

A veil drawn low across our eyes.

A prince once robed in jewelled grace,

Was stripped by storm and nature's face.

But in a hut with woven thread,

He met the self he thought was dead.

He saw a man in patched attire,

Whose smile was warm, whose gaze held fire.

Each seam a tale, each tear a song—

A soul that knew where hearts belong.

We wear our stories not in gold,

But in the way our hands can hold.

Not in the shimmer made to show,

But in the stillness, we let it glow.

For robes will fade, and crowns will rust,

But grace is sewn in love and trust.

What clothes the soul, no eye can see—

And that alone makes one truly free.

As the breeze rustled through the garden, Jahnavi looked up with curiosity in her eyes and asked, "Does a house shelter the body, or is it meant to echo the inner sanctuary of the soul?"

The monk said, almost in a whisper, as if unearthing a sacred tale from the quiet earth itself:

"Once, in a far-off valley where the winds whispered ancient secrets, there lived a master architect. He built mansions—palaces adorned with marble floors, high domes, and stained glass that caught the morning sun like jewels. Kings came to him to build their dreams. Yet, in the quiet of the night, he often sat alone on his cold veranda, feeling strangely homeless.

One day, after a long illness took his beloved wife, he left everything behind and wandered. Hungry, tired, and heartbroken, he stumbled upon a small cottage nestled between two hills. There, an old couple lived. Their house was humble—clay walls, a thatched roof, and no decoration except the warmth that seemed to glow from every corner. He was invited in with smiles, fed with love, and given a corner to rest. That night, though he lay on a straw mat, he slept more deeply than he had in years.

Over time, he helped the couple mend their fence, patch the roof, and plant vegetables in the garden. And slowly, he began to understand. A house is not four walls and a ceiling—it is the echo of presence, the scent of shared laughter, the stillness where souls can breathe. A house, when built only for the body, becomes a shelter. But when built with care, presence, and love—it mirrors the sanctuary within."

He looked at Jahnavi, his voice now as still as the banyan tree nearby.

"Stone shelters the body. But the soul finds its shelter in presence, love, silence, and truth. The house outside is but a shadow—what matters is what it reflects within."

As the golden sun dipped behind the hills and the shadows lengthened in the monk's garden, the children sat in quiet reflection after a day of laughter and learning. Hitesh, he gently tugged at the sleeve of his embroidered kurta and asked, "When clothing becomes identity, have we clothed the self—or concealed it?"

The monk turned, brushing dust from his robe, and his gaze held the weight of many lifetimes.

He spoke slowly, as if each word had to pass through the needle of remembrance.

"There was once a young prince," the monk began, "raised in silks so fine they glimmered like moonlight. From the time he could walk, he wore the weight of expectation—every colour he wore declared his rank, every thread whispered of pride. His robes became his reflection, and soon, he no longer knew where the fabric ended and the self began."

"One day, curious to know the world beyond the palace gates, he stepped out in disguise. Wearing the coarse tunic of a wanderer, he passed unnoticed through villages, forests, and mountains. At first, he missed the glances, the bows, the deference. But slowly, as days turned to weeks, he began to see—eyes that met his not with fear or calculation, but with truth. A potter gave him water. A child gave him a smile. A blind man mistook him for a beggar and offered him half a loaf of bread."

"He felt…seen. Not for his robe, his status, or his name. But for something raw, real, unnamed. It frightened him—and freed him. In the absence of costume, the prince met the presence."

The monk looked around at the children, their eyes wide.

"Clothing can express—but it can also imprison. When we wear it to honour a moment, it's a celebration. But when we wear it to mask our fear, to shape how the world sees us, or to hide our own emptiness, it becomes a veil—not just over our bodies, but over our being."

"True identity," he added gently, "is naked, not in body, but in essence. And that which is eternal in you cannot be stitched, tailored, or torn. It only reveals itself when you are brave enough to stand unclothed before truth."

The garden fell silent—not out of solemnity, but a shared reverence. Hitesh looked down at his kurta, then up at the monk—and smiled. It was not the smile of one who had found all answers, but of one who had found the courage to begin seeking differently.

.

CHAPTER XIV

Roots and Wings

"To be a parent is to love without grasping, to guide without binding, to bless without owning."

– Shree Shambav

The Unseen Bow:

The day was bright, the sun casting golden streaks through the monastery courtyard. The bell had just sounded for mid-meal silence, but Vasudevan, unable to hold back the question rising in his chest, turned to the Monk and asked, "What is parenthood? How should a parent truly be toward a child? What is the real responsibility of a parent?"

The Monk closed his eyes, as if listening for an answer whispered not from his mind, but from the long memory of the soul.

"Let me tell you a story," he said softly. "Not of a king, nor of gods, but of a man... and a bow."

A Bow and an Arrow

There once was a skilled archer who carved his bow from the oldest tree in the forest—a tree that had survived fire, flood, and time itself. He loved the bow not just for its strength, but for how it bent to his will, how it held the line he drew.

He had one arrow—his only child.

Every day, he polished the shaft, shaped the tip, and straightened the feathers. He dreamed of its flight, of the mark it would strike. He taught it the winds, the angles, the patience of the pull. He believed his care, his control, his corrections—were all love.

One day, the arrow slipped from his fingers—not when he intended, not toward the target he imagined. It flew wildly into the unknown, vanishing into the woods. He ran for days, searching, weeping not just from loss, but from shattered pride.

When he finally found the arrow, it was in the hands of a stranger— Not broken, not lost—but painted with colours unknown to him. It had pierced not a bullseye, but a tree that bore fruit he had never tasted.

"I am not the archer," he whispered. "I was only the bow."

The Monk Turned to Vasudevan and Spoke

"Parenthood," he said gently, "is not a sculptor imposing form upon clay—it is a gardener, kneeling before a seed they do not fully understand."

He paused.

"Your child is not your reflection—they are the sunbeam caught briefly in your hand. You do not own the light. You only hold space for it to shine."

"You may give your body, your wisdom, your protection—but their soul?" "That belongs to the river of life that flows through them, not from you."

The Mirror and the Window

Most parents, the Monk explained, look at their children as mirrors—hoping to see their own dreams, ideals, and pride reflected back. But children are not mirrors. They are windows to a world beyond our comprehension. To stare into that window and demand it show you your own face—is to miss the sky behind it.

A Home Worn by Silence

Let me narrate one more story…

There was once a man who had built a house not with bricks alone, but with rules, silence, and routines carved sharp like the edges of stone. He was a widowed father—once gentle, now hardened by grief, and fearful of the world that had already taken too much from him.

His daughter, barely a teenager, was all he had left. And so he loved her the only way he knew how—with protection disguised as control, with care cloaked in commands. Her days were scheduled, her speech measured, her laughter often hushed. He believed that if he could shape her life into neat patterns, the chaos that stole his beloved wife would never return.

His love wore the garments of discipline—ironed collars of expectation, sleeves rolled with sacrifice, and the unspoken belief that love must shield, even if it suffocates.

But the daughter… She was not born of silence, but of song. Not made for stillness, but for sky. She began to push back—first in defiance, then in retreat. Words turned into slammed doors. Smiles became sarcasm. Her presence was now a flicker behind closed curtains.

He mistook her distance for rebellion. She mistook his control for rejection.

And then, one stormy evening—words erupted like thunder. Accusations, disappointments, old griefs reawakened. "You don't see me!" she screamed. "You don't let me breathe!" "You are all I have left," he shouted back, voice breaking. "I cannot lose you too!"

The silence that followed wasn't peace. It was the cracking of something sacred.

And before dawn, she was gone.

A note left behind said nothing of anger. Only one line: "I need to find my voice… before I forget it exists."

Rain fell that night as if the sky wept on his behalf. Time stood still. The house echoed with an unbearable stillness, not because she wasn't there, but because he realised—perhaps she had never felt truly seen.

The Father's Search: A Mirror Shattered

Days turned to weeks. He searched for her—in temples, train stations, shelters, forests. Each place he visited showed him not her, but himself.

In a temple, he saw a statue of a mother and child—free, playful. In the forest, he watched a bird teach its young to fly by letting go. At a homeless shelter, he met a girl about his daughter's age. She asked him, "Would you have loved her if she didn't become what you hoped?"

The question shattered something inside.

He returned home, not to the house—but to her room. It was as she left it—messy, alive, full of things he never took time to understand.

On the wall, he saw a drawing— A girl with open wings, flying above a cage. Beneath it, in small handwriting: "A house is not a home if I must shrink to fit it."

And then… he wept. Not just for her absence, but for how little he had truly listened—not with his ears, but with his soul.

The Return: No Words, Just Presence

She came back at dawn.

Not triumphant, not defeated. Just… changed. Mud clung to her feet. Her eyes no longer flinched at his gaze. She had found something in the world that no room of rules could give her—a voice.

He opened the door. She walked in. No apologies. No demands.

She sat beside him under the old tree in their backyard. He didn't ask where she'd gone. She didn't explain.

They held hands.

The silence this time wasn't emptiness. It was a prayer.

Letting Go of the Sculptor's Chisel

In that silence, something bloomed.

He realised he had not failed as a father because he couldn't control her. He failed because he thought parenthood was creation, when it was always companionship. He had tried to sculpt a statue when he was meant to tend a garden. To shape her identity, when he should have been shelter for its unfolding.

She was not his to define. She was not a legacy. She was a soul, with her own stars to follow.

Monk said, "A house made of silence can protect, but it cannot nourish. Walls may keep danger out—but they can also keep life from entering. And love, true love, is not control masked as care—but the courage to witness another become what even you did not expect."

After a long, thoughtful silence, the monk spoke—not with explanation, but with a verse that echoed like wind through still branches.

Your loving child, a fleeting reflection,

Not of your making, but Life's profound selection.

Daughters and sons of a cosmic design,

Longing for their essence, a destiny enshrined.

Through you they come, yet not from you,

With you, yet belonging to a journey they pursue.

In your care, their bodies find reprieve,

Yet their souls, like rivers, weave and heave.

Guide them, you may, with love untold,

Sacrifice your essence, and a story unfolds.

But thoughts, like whispers of the distant breeze,

Belong to them, dancing through life's mysteries.

A protector of bodies, a guardian strong,

Their souls, like melodies, have their own song.

Predestined paths in the tapestry of fate,

A guide you are, at the mercy of life's debate.

Strive to learn, to evolve, to grow,

Yet let them be, let their unique rivers flow.

For life, a river ceaselessly winding,

Carries sorrows, joys, a continuum binding.

Live not in the shadows of yesterday's pain,

Look beyond, where tomorrow's dreams reign.

You are a bow, your children living arrows,

Guided by destiny, through life's vast meadows.

Divine marks upon the infinite's map,

Bent by the Almighty, in destiny's lap.

The arrow flies, swift and far,

Yet the stable bow bears its own stellar scar.

For in the flight, love transcends the bow,

An eternal dance, as destinies bestow.

Your loving child, not truly your own,

A cosmic creation, in life's grand cyclone.

The monk looked up, eyes soft with memory. *"This is the journey of every parent,"* he said. *"Not to possess,* *but to protect. Not to mould, but to witness. To love deeply… and let go gently."*

The monk smiled gently, as if the silence between verses held its own truth. Then he continued, his voice softer, deeper:

In the hush of wonder, young Aadhya asked,

"Why care for the old—so weary, so masked?"

The monk, whose gaze held time's tender trace,

Spoke softly of love and life's sacred grace.

"When you speak of mothers, Aadhya dear,

Let your words be wrapped in reverent cheer.

We call them burdens, fragile, slow—

Forgetting the seeds they helped us sow."

"Their dreams lie buried in our careless sighs,

In children, they are raised to touch the skies.

We owe them more than glances brief—

We owe them honour, balm for grief."

"Even in quarrels or silence deep,

Their blessings guard us in waking and sleep.

Their joy is woven in our ascent,

Their worth, beyond what words have meant."

"They are lighthouses when the storms appear,

The steady flame that draws us near.

A child may shine, but let it be known—

Parents, too, are stars full-grown."

"They are not weak, but wisdom crowned,

Not fading, but in love profound.

Not burden, but the strength behind—

The hands that shaped the soul and mind."

"Let them not fade at life's dimming light,

But be honoured still in morning's bright.

A home without elders is hollow, unclear—

Like a tree without roots or seasons near."

"They are the hues in life's design,

The butterflies that bless and shine.

A house without them sings a plea—

From cradle to grave, they hold the key."

"So hold them close through dusk and dawn,

For their breath lingers when we've moved on.

In their arms, your own dreams grew—

They are life's well, ever deep and true."

The monk then bowed, his voice grown still,

As if the earth itself bent to his will.

And in that moment, Aadhya knew—

To honour them was to honour what's true.

When he finished, his eyes lingered on the sky as if remembering every parent who had ever loved in silence.

"To honour those who came before us is not tradition—it is awakening," he said. *"For in their sacrifices, we glimpse the soul of love—endless, unseen, and unwavering."*

After a brief pause, the question lingered in the monk's stillness like incense in a quiet shrine.

Arjun's voice had trembled not from doubt, but from the weight of his own fatherhood—two children, one a wanderer of wild dreams, the other, silent and guarded like an unopened book.

He asked, almost to himself: "Is parenthood the art of shaping a life—or the surrender to let life shape itself through you?"

The monk gently looked up. His eyes, softened by years of seeing beyond what is spoken, held a flicker of fire and forgiveness.

He nodded slowly and began.

The Potter's Hands and the River's Way

"There once lived a potter," the monk said, "whose hands were known across the region. Clay obeyed him. He would mould it into urns that held rainwater, bowls that sang when struck, and lamps that cradled light like prayer.

One day, a traveller came to him and said, 'Make me a vessel that will last forever—unbreakable, unchanging, eternal.'

The potter smiled, picked up clay, and began his work. For days, he shaped, re-shaped, paused, and listened—not to the traveller, but to the clay.

'You see,' he finally said, handing the traveller a bowl, 'I do not shape the clay alone. I only help it become what it already longs to be.'

The traveller frowned, unimpressed. 'But it's imperfect. See the curve? The edge is not exact.'

The potter only bowed. 'So is life. It was not made to be exact—it was made to flow.'"

The monk looked at Arjun now—not with answers, but with presence.

"You ask if parenthood is shaping or surrender. But Arjun, can a potter command the river?

A child is not a slab of stone to be carved into your dream. They are more like a seed, carrying their own shape within, and you are the soil—rich, warm, patient. You cannot decide what tree they become, but you can choose whether they bloom in your care or wither under your shadow."

He leaned closer.

"Parenthood is not the pride of creation, but the humility of presence. Yes, there is guidance—like the potter's fingers. But there is also letting go—like the river, who never clutches the leaf but carries it gently forward."

A Pause, Then Insight

The wind rustled the leaves overhead, like applause that had learned to whisper.

Arjun sat back, eyes glistening—not with grief, but with release.

He had spent years fearing he'd failed to shape his children "right." But now, he saw they were not his reflection to be perfect. They were their own sunrise, and he—the horizon that held them while they rose.

The Monk said softly, "Parenthood is not the shaping of another's life. It is the sacred art of surrender—of being the earth beneath their roots and the sky above their dreams. Of offering them a home, not a mould."

And in that silence, Arjun's heart found what he had never sought: peace not in control, but in reverence.

Lavanya asked, "Can true parenting begin only when we learn to see the divine in our children, not our reflection?"

The question did not float—it rooted itself in the quiet space between them.

The Monk only looked up—eyes soft, breath still. In that stillness, Lavanya felt what she had not yet understood: that the most profound answers are not heard, but remembered.

The Mirror and the Flame

The monk finally spoke, not as a teacher—but as a witness.

"There once was a mother who raised her son like a mirror.

She dressed him in the colours she loved. Taught him the words she wished she'd spoken. Praised him when he reflected her strength, and corrected him when he echoed her fears.

He obeyed—at first. But with each passing year, his spirit grew restless. He longed not to reflect, but to burn—to blaze in the world as his own flame.

When he turned eighteen, he left home. He did not run from love, but from expectation disguised as love.

Years later, he returned—not with success, but with sorrow. Life had scarred him, softened him, shown him truths beyond books.

She wept—not for the lost years, but for the lost seeing.

'I thought I was raising a mirror,' she whispered, 'but you were always a star. I just didn't know how to look up.'

The son knelt and held her hand. 'You were the ground beneath me, Ma. I only wished you'd seen I wasn't meant to reflect—but to radiate.'"

The Monk Turned to Lavanya

"We often say our child," he said, "but the child is not ours. Not really. They come through us—not from us. They are entrusted, not owned. And the moment we start seeing them as divine—not an extension of our ego or unfulfilled dreams—we become sacred witnesses to their becoming."

He paused.

"To see the divine in a child is to remember they have a path of their own. Our role is not to design their destiny, but to bless it. Not to command, but to hold space. Not to fill them, but to stand in reverence as they unfold."

The Garden and the Sunlight

"Think of a garden," the monk continued. "Each plant needs a different kind of care. Some lean toward the sun, others grow in shade. You cannot make a lotus bloom like a rose. To demand that is not parenting—it is spiritual blindness."

"The sun never tells the flower how to bloom. It only shines."

A Silent Benediction

The wind whispered through the leaves above them.

Lavanya looked up at the tree's vast canopy.

No more questions arose. No more answers were needed.

No more commands. No more rebellion. Only presence.

CHAPTER XV

The Threads We Leave Behind

"True sacrifice is not what is given up, but what is given over—to love, to truth, to something greater than self."

– Shree Shambav

It was raining—soft, rhythmic, unhurried. The kind of rain that does not drench but whispers. Children were outside, their laughter echoing like temple bells in the open air. They were chasing paper boats—tiny dreams folded in fragile hope—riding the rivers formed on temple steps and stone paths.

The monk sat quietly under the awning, watching them—still, smiling. His gaze was not fixed on the boats but on the joy that pulled them forward.

Aadhya, her eyes glowing with mischief, tugged at his robe. "Come play, Baba! You always sit and smile. Join us today."

The monk raised an eyebrow in mock seriousness. "Me? Should I sail a boat or become one?" The children giggled. Aadhya insisted, "Yes! You be the river."

Elders sitting nearby chuckled, some whispering how odd yet beautiful it was—to see a sage of silence ready to step into puddles.

With a gentle nod, the monk stood, folded his robe above the ankles, and joined them. He cupped his hand, shaped a boat from a dried leaf, and set it into the stream beside the children's crafts.

The rain slowed. The clouds softened. Even the water seemed to pause—not to stop the flow, but to honour a moment.

The Question That Opened the Soul

Radhya, now a mother, stood on the veranda, watching the scene. The monk's laughter, light as a flute, triggered something deep in her.

She was once a girl with paper boats, once a daughter who believed her mother's worn hands were magic. She remembered her mother walking barefoot through muddy fields, always giving, always quiet.

Tears welled in her eyes—not from sadness, but recognition. After a while, she whispered, almost to herself but loud enough for the monk to hear:

"What is sacrifice? Is there a difference between giving… and true sacrifice? What makes it sacred?"

A Parched Beginning

The monk dried his hands slowly on the edge of his robe. His voice, when it came, was soft as the rain just passed.

"Let me tell you a story, Radhya… In a village long forgotten by maps and time, there came a drought. The skies withheld their tears, and the earth cracked open like a broken heart. Wells turned into mirrors of despair. Trees became ghosts. Fields, empty pages."

"In that village lived an old woman—frail, poor, nameless to most. She had nothing… except a small clay bowl of grain, saved over days like whispered prayers. One day, she heard of a child—burning with fever, his family gone, lying alone. She took her bowl, walked through the heat, and gave it all. No one saw. No one praised her. She returned to her hut and closed her eyes for the last time."

"Years passed. Rain returned. So did people. That child—he grew. He became a healer, guided by a wandering sage. When the village was struck again—this time by plague—he returned, saving hundreds. They called him a saviour. But he remembered the taste of that grain, the hand that fed him when the world turned away."

"Only two elders spoke her name when she was gone. Her hut had crumbled. But her sacrifice… it lived on, like a thread in every breath he healed."

The Silence That Followed

No one spoke for a while.

The monk didn't need to explain the story. It had entered not through their ears, but through the space between their ribs—where soul and memory meet.

The children stopped playing, standing quietly beside the elder now. Even they understood in their own way: that some boats sail on water, and some on love left behind.

The monk finally added, gently:

"Giving is often a transaction—an exchange the ego records. Sacrifice… true sacrifice… is when the self is no longer part of the offering. It is not given from us. It flows through us."

"Like a silkworm weaving its own end, not knowing that in its vanishing, it births beauty. So too are we invited—not to be noticed, but to be woven into someone else's becoming."

In the cocoon's embrace, a story unfolds,

A tale of sacrifice by a silkworm told.

In the silken threads, its essence spun,

A journey began with the setting sun.

A creature small, in quiet repose,

Silken whispers, the cocoon bestows.

Threads of sacrifice, each strand a prayer,

Weaving dreams, suspended in the air.

The mulberry leaves, a humble fare,

Yet, within the worm, resilience is rare.

Silent martyr in the moon's soft glow,

A sacrifice woven, a life to bestow.

Metamorphosis, a cosmic ballet,

A silkworm's fate, in silk array.

In the loom of time, destiny's weaver,

A sacrifice profound, a silk achiever.

As fibres bind, a tapestry grand,

The silkworm's sacrifice, a silent stand.

Each silk strand, a whispering hymn,

In the loom of life, a sacrifice is slim.

The loom's dance, a rhythmic trance,

Threads entwining a delicate advance.

The silkworm's sacrifice, a silent plea,

In the silk's embrace, a legacy.

O silkworm, in your sacrifice find,

A metaphor for the human mind.

In life's cocoon, we too transform,

Sacrifices made in silence, warm.

In threads of hope, resilience spun,

A silken journey, just begun.

For in each sacrifice, a lesson learned,

In the tapestry of life, the silkworms earned.

"Sacrifice," he said, "is not to be seen. It is to be woven."

"Some offer themselves loudly, and some vanish into the fabric of life."

"The world may forget the weaver, but the warmth of the cloth remembers."

Apoorva's voice pierced the silence—not with doubt, but with quiet wonder.

"What is the difference between a sacrifice made for validation and one offered in stillness, without name?"

The monk looked at her—not just at her face, but through it, as if reading the layers of her soul. He did not answer immediately. Some questions are not answered with explanations, but with a journey.

He finally spoke, not to explain, but to take them somewhere.

The Two Lamps:

"Let me tell you about two lamps," he said. "Both burn through the long night, offering light to passersby on a dark village road."

"The first lamp is proud. It looks at each traveller and thinks: 'They see me. They walk because of me. I am the guide. I am the source.' It shines brighter when watched. But if no one passes, its flame flickers with doubt."

"The second lamp burns quietly. It does not need eyes to see it, nor praise to fuel it. It was lit not to be admired, but because darkness simply asked for light."

"By morning, both lamps are spent. But the second leaves behind warmth in the hearts of those who walked silently beside it. The first leaves only the memory of its need to be seen."

The Insight Beneath the Flame

The monk's gaze deepened.

"Apoorva, sacrifice made for validation wears a mask—it is generosity that seeks applause, giving that collects receipts. It is still a gift, yes—but one that circles back to the giver."

"But sacrifice in stillness? That is devotion without an audience. It is when the self dissolves into the act—when the doer vanishes, and only the deed remains. No name. No credit. Just a ripple sent out into the world, without waiting for the wave to return."

The monk smiled.

"True sacrifice," he said, "is not remembered in marble or song. It becomes a part of the air—unseen, yet essential. Like the silkworm's thread, like the water hidden in the roots—its purpose is not to be noticed, but to nourish life in silence."

Surya asked: "Can sacrifice become sacred only when it leaves behind the self that offers it?"

The question did not break the silence—it deepened it.

The monk looked toward the distant hills, where clouds moved like wandering monks themselves—weightless, unpossessed. He let the silence stretch, not to delay, but to invite everyone into the depth of the inquiry.

Then he spoke softly, as if sharing something sacred, not merely true.

The Story of the River and the Stone

"Let me tell you the tale of a river and a stone," he began. "There was once a great stone that sat in the heart of a dry valley. Proud and ancient, it longed to offer something meaningful to the world. 'Let me shape the valley,' it said. 'Let me carve the land in my image.'"

"But it was too still, too rigid. The valley remained untouched."

"Then came the river, small at first, just a whisper of water. It didn't try to carve anything. It simply moved—giving, flowing, surrendering its shape, letting the land guide its path. Day by day, year by year, it wore the stone down—not with force, but with patience. In time, it shaped a fertile valley. Crops grew. Life returned. And the river had no name."

The monk looked at Surya and continued:

"The stone wanted to give while remaining itself—solid, seen, intact. The river ceased to be so that something greater could live."

The Insight Beneath the Surface

"You asked if sacrifice becomes sacred only when the self is left behind. Let me offer you this: A sacred act begins where the ego ends. When there's no longer a 'someone' doing, just the doing itself, that is where grace is born."

"The moment you say, 'I sacrificed,' the sacredness becomes shadowed by the self. But when the self dissolves into the act, like the river into the valley, it is no longer 'your' sacrifice. It is life giving to life. It is love wearing no label, flowing without memory."

A Whisper, Not a Proclamation

The monk's voice was now quieter than the breeze.

"True sacrifice doesn't look back. It doesn't seek recognition or even remembrance. It's like a tree that blossoms unseen, dropping fruit into a stranger's hand. It is sacred because it is selfless, and it is selfless because it forgets the self entirely."

The sun broke through the thinning clouds. Children's laughter echoed in the background like a hymn carried by wind. And in that moment, no one clapped, no one spoke. But something sacred had been felt—not taught.

Sacrifice had revealed itself—not as loss, but as transformation.

CHAPTER XVI

The Sea Within Us

"Only empty hands can touch the divine—only the open heart can give without bleeding."

– Shree Shambav

It was a bright day, and the breeze wandered playfully through the village, carrying with it the scent of wild jasmine and the soft laughter of children. Nearby, leaves rustled like quiet whispers, and the sky stretched vast and unburdened above.

Beneath the ancient banyan tree, the Monk sat in stillness—his robe gathered at his side, his eyes resting not on any one thing, but seeing everything. He watched the world with the gaze of one who had let go of needing to name it.

Birds flew low across the fields. A potter passed with a clay jug balanced on his head. The moment was ordinary—and yet sacred.

Satya, seated cross-legged among the others, broke the silence—not with urgency, but with wonder.

"What is desire?" he asked. "How does it become a need? And how does that need slip silently into greed?"

The Monk turned to him slowly, a smile rising like the morning sun on his face. His eyes held the weight of stories yet untold. After a moment's pause, he looked toward the distant hills as if the wind might answer first—and then he began to speak.

"Let me tell you a tale—not just of sea and storms, but of the tides that live within us all."

The Fisherman and the Sea of Longing

There once lived a fisherman by a quiet bay—his name lost to time, but his story, like the sea, still speaks. He rose before dawn, not to chase riches, but to meet the morning tide like an old friend. Each cast of his net was not for gain, but gratitude. He would whisper to the waters, "Only what is needed—no more."

In those early days, the sea fed him like a mother—modest fish, enough for his family, a few to share. He would sit on the shore after the sun had climbed, watching the ripples dance, letting the salt wind wash through the creases of his brow. His joy was quiet, like dew upon a leaf—unnoticed, but whole.

But then came whispers. A traveller spoke of markets in the cities. "You have the sea," he said. "You can be rich." And thus, the seed of desire took root—not evil, not wrong, just…restless.

At first, the fisherman fished a little more. "I'll save some," he told himself. "For the future. For safety." His neighbours praised him. The coins clinked like music in his pouch. What once was enough became too little. Need, once a gentle guest, turned into a master at his table. And so, need gave birth to greed—not as a monster with teeth, but as a friend with a thousand reasonable justifications.

He built a second boat, then a third. He hired others to cast wider nets. He no longer spoke to the sea—only commanded it. "Give me more," he would mutter, "I have mouths to feed. A name to build."

And then came the storm.

The Breaking

It arrived without warning—sky cracked open, waves rose like judgment. His boat, once the pride of the coast, splintered like a toy beneath a child's wrath. He clung to driftwood, broken not just in body but in belief. For the first time in years, he listened—to the sea's roaring silence.

For three days, he floated—no riches, no servants, no nets. Just the sound of his own breath and the slow dying of all he had built.

Then, out of the mist, came a small canoe. A fisherman from a nearby village—a stranger, poor, unknown. He pulled him aboard, gave him his last dry bread, wrapped him in his own cloth, and paddled him to shore.

The next morning, the stranger left without asking for thanks, but before he departed, he placed in the fisherman's hand a simple fishing net—his only one.

"You once knew the sea," the man said softly. "Perhaps now you'll remember it."

The Return

The man, humbled and quiet, returned to his bay. He no longer built fleets. He no longer counted coins. He cast the net like a prayer. Sometimes it came back empty. Sometimes full. He smiled either way.

He gave away much of his catch. To widows. To children. To those who reminded him of his former self—ambitious, hungry, and lost.

He no longer fished to conquer the sea—but to be in harmony with it.

And slowly, the village changed. Greed softened. The waters grew kinder. The shore sang a different song.

The Monk's voice fell silent, like the hush after a wave breaks.

"Desire," he said, "is not your enemy. It is like wind—it can lift a sail or topple a ship."

"Need," he continued, "is the space between contentment and hunger. But greed—that arises when we forget we are guests, not owners, of this world."

He looked at Satya and the others, their eyes wide in the quiet that followed.

"The sea within us is always moving. But only when we learn to row with humility, and anchor with gratitude, can we truly sail."

Beneath the dark blue waves I drift,

Carried by tides I do not name,

Desires rise like moons above me,

And fall, like stars, the same.

Oh, the tide is full; the moon looks bright,

Stars glimmering vastly in the sky,

The ocean meets the moon-blanched land,

Waves begin and cease continuously,

As our desire begins and ceases continuously,

Does it have a peaceful sleep ever then?

Desires are like waves that begin and cease,

It begins with a high-grating roar,

And then ceases with a shaky slow rhythm,

The eternal note of sadness,

Does it have a peaceful sleep ever then?

We are like boats, sailing in desires' sway,

Leading our lives according to our wants,

Running all our lives behind those desires,

Does it have a peaceful sleep ever then?

In our blowing breeze of youth's embrace,

We get attached to the fluttering love,

We cherish and enjoy the precious moments,

Feeling we've attained serenity and bliss,

Does it have a peaceful sleep ever then?

If I have attained serenity and bliss,

Why does this youth disappear so fast?

Why have desires turned into painful chains?

Will I regain my youth and happiness?

Does it have a peaceful sleep ever then?

Will my heart blossom, filled with fragrance sweet,

Will my mind hold beautiful memories close?

Is old age a curse or wisdom delight?

I'm unsure, waiting and watching,

Will I have a peaceful sleep ever then?

When a hailstorm strikes the raging sea,

How can I sail calmly and safely?

All I realise is sorrow's income,

All my happiness feels like an expenditure.

Will I have a peaceful sleep ever then?

I yearn to break free from all these bondages,

Must I wait for the right time to come?

Is there still work left for me to complete?

I've realised the present is a fleeting dream,

Will I have a peaceful sleep ever then?

What calculations have I made for my life?

To keep it safe, and to keep it happy?

Who knows? Fate has different calculations,

Will I have a peaceful sleep ever then?

Deep beneath the dark blue waves.

Perhaps peace is not the end of longing,

But the quiet shore it leads us to,

Where I no longer chase the rising tide,

But let its rhythm carry me through.

A moment of stillness.

The rustling of leaves was the only reply for a while, as if the wind itself paused to listen. A sparrow fluttered onto a stone nearby and then flew off again—like a thought that comes and goes without attachment.

Ramesh spoke softly, as though voicing a question he had carried for years:

"Can desire be a sacred current—if it flows without the thirst to possess?"

The monk's gaze rested on the river in the distance, glimmering beneath the golden sun. He didn't answer immediately. His silence was not the absence of speech—it was the presence of contemplation.

After a while, he said:

"When desire flows like a river nourishing both shores, it becomes sacred. But when it seeks to dam the world for itself—it drowns all it touches."

The disciples leaned in, knowing a story was coming—not just from his lips, but from his life.

The Parable of the Twin Rivers

Once, in a land of vast plains and fertile earth, there were two rivers born of the same mountain—twin sisters, flowing side by side.

The first river flowed freely. She watered forests, gave life to fields, and quenched the thirst of wanderers. She never paused to count what she gave. Flowers bloomed along her banks, and animals rested in her shade. The people called her Ananda—the joyous one.

The second river, seeing how much her sister gave away, grew anxious.

"What if I lose myself giving to others?" she thought. "I must build banks higher, tighter—contain all I am, so I may be greater."

She built dams and walls. At first, her waters shimmered with pride. But slowly, her current slowed, her song grew silent, and her once-lush banks turned dry. The life that once danced beside her vanished. The people called her Dukha—the sorrowing one.

One day, a great storm came. The dam broke. In her final surge, she flooded everything—even those she once tried to impress. Her thirst to possess left only ruin.

The first river still flowed, quietly, endlessly—alive in the joy of giving.

The monk paused. His eyes were soft, not with pity—but with understanding.

“Desire is not wrong,” he said, “but its direction defines its nature. Let it flow outward, and it blesses all. Let it circle endlessly within, and it becomes a whirlpool.”

Ramesh bowed his head, not in shame, but in realisation.

The breeze stirred once again. A leaf danced gently to the earth. No one spoke. They didn’t need to. The river nearby continued to flow—quietly, without need for applause.

A hush fell over the gathering. The river sang softly in the distance, and a few dry leaves stirred across the temple stone.

Bharati’s voice, gentle yet piercing, carried the weight of a lifetime of giving.

“What transforms giving from obligation into liberation?” she asked.

The monk closed his eyes, not in retreat, but as one who listens beyond words. For a few moments, he said nothing. The silence felt sacred—like the space between breaths when one is most alive.

Then, with a tone as light as a falling feather, he answered:

"When you give not from surplus or guilt, but from presence and joy— Then your gift becomes light, not weight."

And as his words settled like morning dew, he began to tell a story.

The Weaver and the Thread of Gold

In a small village nestled between emerald hills, there lived an old woman named Zoya, known to all as the Weaver. Her fingers were bent with age, but her cloth was softer than any silk, more vibrant than even royal garments.

People said she used enchanted thread. But none knew the truth.

Each day, Zoya would sit before her loom, not for profit, but for prayer. She wove not because she had to, but because she loved the feel of thread moving through her fingers—like a hymn whispered through action.

One day, the king's minister arrived in the village, seeking cloth for the Queen's coronation. Zoya offered him a shawl—woven in deep blues and golden strands.

The minister admired it. "How much gold must we offer you for this?" he asked.

Zoya smiled and shook her head. "I cannot sell this, nor can I gift it in obligation. This was woven for the woman who sits by the temple each dusk, shivering. It belongs to her."

The minister protested. "But she is a beggar!"

Zoya replied, "Then she needs warmth more than your Queen needs grandeur."

He asked, "Why not weave more—for us, for others?"

She said quietly, "I do not weave with my hands alone. I weave with my soul. When that is spent, the cloth is empty, no matter how fine."

That evening, she wrapped the shawl gently around the beggar woman's shoulders. The woman didn't speak—her eyes shimmered with something wordless, like dusk itself embracing light.

And as the Queen stood that week, draped in royal silk, the beggar sat in warmth, draped in love.

The monk opened his eyes. His voice was barely more than a whisper:

"Giving from obligation is like pouring water into a desert that never blooms. But giving from presence is rain that nourishes both the earth and the cloud."

Bharati sat still. Something in her chest—a tension long held—unwound. She thought of all she had given in her life—some in love, some in fear, and some just to be seen.

Now, she saw the difference.

The sun lowered, casting long golden shadows. A child brought the monk a flower—unasked, unmeasured. He smiled and tucked it behind his ear. No thanks. No transaction. Just grace offered... and grace received.

CHAPTER XVII

The Meadow Within

"When the eyes soften and the heart listens, the whole world sings in silent splendour."

– Shree Shambav

The morning light spilled like gold across the open meadows. Wildflowers swayed in the breeze, each one radiant in its simple, unknowing grace. Children laughed as they chased butterflies, their joy as unbound as the wind. Elders walked slowly behind, smiling at the innocence that had once been theirs.

Among them walked the Monk, silent as the sky, his steps soft on the earth as though he remembered it was sacred.

A little girl, Aadhya, tugged at his robe.

Her cheeks were flushed from running, her eyes curious like a newly opened bud.

"Monk," she asked with childlike sincerity, "what is happiness?"

The monk paused. He looked out at the meadow, the blossoms, the bees humming their holy tune. Then he turned to her, eyes glowing gently.

"Come," he said, and sat beneath a flowering tree.

As the others gathered around, he began a story.

The Mirror in the Garden

There once lived a woman named Amara who had the most beautiful garden in her village. People came from far and wide to marvel at her roses, her tulips, and the vines that kissed the sky. Every flower bloomed in her presence—as if even the earth loved her touch.

But Amara herself was never seen smiling.

Each morning, she would walk past her mirror, sighing. "I must grow more beautiful flowers," she would whisper, "for maybe then I'll feel beautiful too."

Seasons passed. Her garden flourished, but she withered. Her body bent, her eyes dimmed. Even the bees stopped dancing around her.

One day, a little boy wandered into her garden. Dirty-faced, barefoot, he gazed at the flowers with awe.

"Are these yours?" he asked.

"Yes," Amara replied.

"They're the happiest flowers I've ever seen."

She sighed. "They are happy because they don't see what I see in the mirror."

The boy tilted his head. "But… they do. That's why they bloom."

She blinked.

He continued, "You care for them. You talk to them. You love them—even when you forget to love yourself. Maybe the mirror isn't broken. Maybe it's just facing the wrong way."

That night, Amara turned the mirror toward her garden.

And for the first time, she saw her reflection not in the glass—but in the joy she had created. In the life she had touched.

She wept—not out of sorrow, but out of release.

And in that moment, a smile finally bloomed… not on her face, but from her soul.

After a still moment, the Monk looked at Aadhya and the others.

He then softly recited:

In the garden of your soul, a tender seed,

Nurture it with love, for that's all you need.

Embrace the art of caring, let joy unfurl,

For within your soul's embrace lies the world.

Self-love, a spark, ignites the way,

A gentle ember, lighting night to day.

Boundless happiness, a path anew,

In the warmth of self-love, find your true view.

Within your embrace, discover grace,

For you are the cosmos in this space.

A microcosm of the grand design,

Reflecting stars in your soul's divine.

What you seek within, you'll find without,

In the depths of self, remove all doubt.

Search within; the answers abide,

For truth and wisdom in you reside.

Let your love be a beacon, shining bright,

Guiding others through the darkest night.

In nature's symphony, find your part,

For in self-acceptance, heal your heart.

In nature's symphony, each creature sings,

Embracing its essence, the joy it brings.

Yet in the human heart, a struggle begins,

To love oneself, where true freedom begins.

So let us learn from nature's song,

To love ourselves, where we belong.

For in the art of nurturing our soul,

Lies the essence of joy, making us whole.

The children sat quiet. Even the butterflies seemed to pause, resting on petals like punctuation marks to a sacred sentence.

The Monk said gently:

"You see, happiness isn't something we chase. It's something we remember. Like a forgotten song that starts playing again when we stop trying to sing louder than our own heart."

He looked at Aadhya.

"You asked what happiness is. It is the smile of a flower blooming simply because it is loved—not because it is perfect."

The breeze stirred again. The meadow shimmered.

And in that moment, even the grown-ups saw the child within them smile.

The Unseen Bloom — On Beauty

After what felt like eternity, Shivanya, a young girl with thoughtful eyes, finally broke the quiet:

"Monk," she asked softly, "what is beauty?"

The Monk opened his eyes slowly and looked at her—not with surprise, but with deep attention.

He didn't speak immediately. Instead, he gazed toward the far hills.

Then he began, his voice like a stream that had known many stones.

The Flower That Faced the Wall

In a kingdom of grand gardens, there lived a royal gardener named Aneesh. His task was to grow the most beautiful flowers for the palace—a task he did with pride and perfection.

Each day, he carefully watered the roses, trimmed the lilies, and whispered to the orchids. The King would walk by and nod in approval, for everything bloomed in divine symmetry.

But behind the garden, where no one visited, stood a cracked wall. And near that wall grew a strange, crooked flower. Its stem was bent, its petals uneven, its colour dull compared to the rest.

Aneesh often ignored it. "What worth is a flower that no one sees?" he thought.

One day, a blind beggar wandered into the garden.

He stopped near the wall, breathing in the air, then sat by the crooked flower and wept softly.

Aneesh, surprised, asked, "Why do you weep near that flower?"

The beggar smiled through tears, "I cannot see the flowers you praise—but this one… this one has the sweetest scent. It reminds me of my mother's sari when she'd hug me as a child. It brings peace to my heart."

Aneesh fell silent.

He realised he had spent a lifetime chasing symmetry and colour—but missed the beauty that needed no eyes. The beauty that was felt, not shown.

From that day on, he tended the crooked flower with care—not for the palace, not for approval—but for the soul it touched.

What makes the blossom pure and bright—

Its colour bold or the scent of night?

Is beauty what the eye can see,

Or what the soul sets truly free?

The mirror shows a flawless face,

But cannot catch a heart's true grace.

The stars may shine with grand display,

Yet kindness lights a truer way.

The mountain dressed in silver snow,

May never tell how winds below,

Have carved its silence, year by year,

With patient storms and falling tear.

A bird that sings with a broken wing,

Still teaches joy in how we sing.

Its song is not in pitch or tone,

But that it dares to sing alone.

So if you seek what beauty means,

Look not in the glass or the magazine.

But in the soul that dares to bloom,

Where no applause, nor eyes, presume.

The Monk looked at Shivanya and said gently, "Beauty is not what draws the eyes—but what awakens the heart. A flower may face a wall its whole life and still carry heaven in its scent."

The children looked around. One pointed to a crooked wildflower growing between two stones.

And somehow, in that quiet moment, it was the most beautiful thing any of them had ever seen.

The Forgotten Joy

The air was thick with stillness, scented with the perfume of wild jasmine. Children played in the distance, their laughter weaving through the trees like a hymn, while old women lit lamps by the temple steps.

The Monk sat on the stone ledge, his robe catching the breeze, his eyes half-closed in listening. Not to the world outside, but to something subtler. Something that danced between the cracks of silence and sound.

After a long pause, he spoke—his voice gentle, as if brushing dust off an old memory.

The Long Road Home

"Once, there was a traveller," the Monk began, "a seeker of joy."

He had wandered across continents—from misty monasteries to bustling cities, from the embrace of lovers to the isolation of desert caves. He meditated with sages, laughed at feasts, and cried alone in forests.

Each new experience promised fulfilment, but each left him emptier than before.

He had tasted pleasures, but they vanished like breath on a mirror.

In time, his footsteps grew weary, not from the distance, but from the weight of his longing. The fire of pursuit became smoke.

So, he returned—not in triumph, but in surrender—to the village where he was born.

It was a small, forgotten place—fields of mustard in bloom, elders humming old songs, and dust that remembered the footprints of ancestors.

One evening, sitting beneath the neem tree of his childhood, he closed his eyes—not to escape, but simply to rest.

A little girl approached, no older than six, her hair in a tangle, her smile wide as dawn. She didn't ask his name or why he looked so tired.

She simply placed a wildflower in his palm and said, "This is for you."

He opened his eyes, looked at the simple blossom—white, imperfect, real. And then, he looked at her smile.

In that moment, time paused.

Not because something extraordinary had happened, but because something eternally ordinary had returned.

He laughed—not a loud laugh, but the soft, trembling laugh of a man who had remembered something sacred he had long forgotten.

He had travelled the world to find joy, only to discover it was never lost. He had only stopped knowing how to see.

The Monk looked up, eyes moist but radiant.

"Happiness," he whispered, "is not found—it is revealed. It is not in the distant star, but in the child's smile, the falling leaf, the warm cup in your hand. Beauty surrounds us like air—we suffer not from its absence, but from blindness."

And as the breeze stirred the grass around them, the following poem unfolded—not as a recital, but as a soul remembering its own forgotten song.

Quiet Enough to See

A gentle hush held the group as they sat around the monk—an unspoken reverence, not for the man, but for the silence that seemed to deepen around him like a sacred well.

Children had stopped playing. Elders leaned in. Even the wind seemed to listen.

It was in that stillness that Jahnavi, with eyes full of wonder and an ache that hadn't found words until now, asked:

"Is beauty something we see—or something we become quiet enough to recognise?"

The monk didn't answer immediately. Instead, he turned to look at the fading light as it kissed the petals of a small wildflower nearby.

A breeze passed. Then he spoke.

The Clay Mirror

"Let me tell you the story of a potter's daughter," the monk said softly.

In a village wrapped in the arms of mountains, a potter lived with his young daughter, Laxmi. She was a quiet child, always covered in specks of clay, always watching. Her father, a master of his craft, shaped pots that were ordinary to others but carried a stillness that made you pause.

People came from faraway towns to buy his work. One day, a merchant asked, "What makes your pots so beautiful?"

The potter smiled. "I don't add beauty—I remove the noise."

The merchant laughed, not understanding.

But Laxmi did.

As she grew, Laxmi too learned the art. She watched how her father touched the clay—not to impose form but to listen to it. He'd often whisper, "Clay already knows what it wants to become. I just help it remember."

But Laxmi struggled. Her pots never turned out right. She mimicked her father's hands, techniques, even his silences—but something was missing.

Frustrated, she wandered into the woods one day. There, beside a brook, she sat down. She didn't shape anything. She didn't think. She just listened—to the sound of water, the rustling leaves, her own breath.

Hours passed like minutes.

Then suddenly, she saw it.

The shape of beauty was not something she could make—it was something she could only recognise when she became quiet enough to receive it.

She rushed back and made a simple bowl. Not ornate. Not symmetrical. But when her father saw it, tears filled his eyes.

"Now," he whispered, "you've truly begun."

The monk paused. His eyes were on the horizon where the sun had just dipped beyond the hills.

"Beauty," he said, turning to Jahnavi, "is not just what we see. It is what sees us when we are still enough to allow it. Most of us are looking with eyes clouded by noise—judgment, hurry, desire. True beauty is not loud; it waits. And we must become quiet enough to recognise it."

The Dusty Mirror

"The heart is like a mirror," he continued. "Over time, it gathers dust—of comparison, fear, ambition, shame. And we stop seeing clearly. But the mirror never loses its power to reflect. Beauty isn't gone—it's simply hidden beneath noise. Silence is the cloth that cleanses it."

A stillness followed. A deeper one than before. As if each listener had been turned inward, toward a forgotten stream in their own soul. No one spoke. Not even Jahnavi. But her eyes shimmered, as though something unseen had finally been recognised.

When We Stop Running

Under a quiet grove, where the trees leaned inward as if sharing secrets, the monk sat surrounded by villagers, travellers, and a few wandering seekers.

Radhya, the quietest among them, had been listening for days. She had journeyed far, not only across valleys but through grief, disappointment, and an ache she couldn't name.

That evening, as the light filtered through the trees, she finally spoke.

"What if happiness is not a pursuit, but the light that dawns when we stop running?"

The monk looked at her—not with surprise, but with the tenderness reserved for those who finally speak from the wound beneath their words.

He nodded, as if he too had once asked the same question in silence.

The Man Who Chased the Sun

"There was once a man," the monk began, "who longed to catch the sun."

He believed that if he could just reach it, just hold a piece of that golden light in his hands, he would be happy forever. So he ran—each morning chasing the sunrise, each evening longing for the fading light. Across mountains, rivers, cities, and deserts, he ran.

Years passed. His feet bled, his breath grew short, and his eyes burned with longing. Yet no matter how far he ran, the sun always remained just beyond his grasp.

One day, lost and exhausted, he collapsed beneath a tree in an unfamiliar village. He could no longer run. He could barely breathe. An old woman walked by and gently placed a bowl of cool water in his hands.

As he drank, he looked up—and saw the sunlight dancing on the leaves above him, shimmering on the water's surface, resting warmly on his face.

It was everywhere.

Not distant. Not hidden.

He hadn't needed to chase it. He had only needed to be still enough to feel it.

"In that moment," the monk said softly, "he wept. For all the years he had spent searching for what had never left him."

Happiness Is Not Elsewhere

The monk turned toward Radhya, his voice like wind brushing over water.

"We are taught that happiness is somewhere ahead—in the next success, the next love, the next version of ourselves. So we run. And in running, we miss the soft miracles unfolding all around us."

"Happiness," he said, "is not a prize for effort. It is the light that dawns when the storm within us stills. It is the scent of wet earth, the kindness of a stranger, the peace of no longer needing to become someone else."

The Sky and the Bird

"The bird does not chase the sky," he said. "It simply spreads its wings and rises. The sky was never separate. It was always there."

"So it is with happiness. It is not something we reach. It is something we return to, when we no longer need to outrun ourselves."

Radhya lowered her gaze, not in shame, but as if her soul had found something too precious for words. A tear traced her cheek, not out of sorrow, but because a burden had quietly slipped away.

She wasn't running anymore.

And in that stillness, something golden opened within her.

CHAPTER XVIII

The Fire That Fades

"Pleasure burns bright, but joy warms slow—choose your fire wisely."

– Shree Shambav

The name Sahasrananda—the one of "a thousand joys"—began to ripple across the kingdom like morning light across still water. What started as whispers in village wells became songs sung in the markets, stories murmured by the elderly, and lullabies in mothers' voices.

The King, a ruler known for his fairness and strength, often ventured across his kingdom in disguise, walking among the people to understand their lives beyond courtly reports. On one such journey, robed as a common traveller with his trusted ministers, he noticed something strange.

In every village he passed, it was not his name they praised, but Sahasrananda's.

"Did you hear what the monk told Kamala when her husband fell ill?" "His words brought my son out of despair." "My crops failed, but he taught me how to smile with the rain." "My daughter sings his verses in the morning—she sleeps more peacefully now."

The King felt an unfamiliar stirring in his chest—was it envy, or fear of irrelevance?

One minister leaned closer and whispered, "Your Majesty… this is not a good sign. The people remember his name more than yours. Today, it is reverence; tomorrow, it may become rebellion. Kings should be the centre of the realm—not wandering monks."

But another minister, older and wiser, responded gently, "My Lord, I have walked these same roads for years. Once, even amidst wealth, I heard only tired complaints. People had full plates but empty eyes. Now… even in drought-struck areas, they greet us with joy. Sahasrananda has given them something we could not: meaning. Not through coin or command—but through presence and peace."

He paused, then added, "He does not seek power, but he has awakened the hearts of your people. That is not a threat—it is a blessing."

The King remained silent. They entered a small village, where laughter echoed around an old tree. Children played barefoot, their joy unburdened. An elderly man with a bent back was reciting a verse the monk had once spoken, and around him villagers sat—not just listening, but living the words.

The King looked at the faces: weathered but serene, lined with labour yet luminous. Something dawned on him—not of fear, but humility.

He turned to his ministers and said softly, "A King rules by law… but a sage rules hearts without throne or sword. Let Sahasrananda be. For he does not diminish my crown—he sanctifies it."

The Smoke and the Flame

The sun had barely risen when the monk Sahasrananda and his quiet band of followers arrived at a dusty village nestled between two dry rivers. The land was tired. Not from drought, but from disconnection. You could feel it in the air—a weariness that clung to the homes like cobwebs.

As they entered the square, the monk saw a group of men gathered under a tree. Empty liquor bottles circled their feet. Cards slapped the stone ground with every bet. Their eyes, glazed and hollow, danced only in the shadow of the next escape. Laughter burst forth, but it was sharp, like broken glass disguised as joy.

Meanwhile, across the village, women hauled water from distant wells, cooked in silence, tended to children, and tilled what little earth they had. Their backs bent, but not their spirits.

One of the elder women, her hands weathered but her voice steady, walked up to the drunkest man and asked, "Why do you waste your breath in drink and dice, while your wife bleeds her hands for food?"

The man let out a loud laugh, the kind that mocks rather than amuses. "You don't understand pleasure," he slurred. "Why break your back when you can drown your pain in taste and thrill? This…"—he held up a bottle—"this is life."

The monk stood silent, his eyes not judging but listening.

Then, a voice—clear, curious—broke the moment. Aadhya, a young girl with large, searching eyes, stood before the monk.

"What is pleasure?" she asked, her voice soft and sincere.

The monk knelt beside her. He picked up a small twig and lit its end with a coal. The fire flared for a moment and then died.

"This," he said, "is pleasure that consumes." He then picked up a lamp and lit its wick. The flame was steady, warm. It lit the faces around it.

"And this," he whispered, "is joy that sustains."

Then Aadhya, an inquisitive child, asked—

"What is a pleasure?" soft and mild.

The monk just smiled, then struck a flame,

And through his words, the wisdom came.

A spark ignites in senses deep,

But leaves the soul alone to weep.

Pleasure calls in golden hue,

Yet vanishes when day is through.

The rose of touch may blush and fade,

Its scent but fleeting, thinly laid.

But joy, a garden grown with care,

Blooms in the heart, ever fair.

Not in the grasp, but in the flow,

Does true delight begin to grow.

Give what you seek, release the chain—

And what remains is bliss through pain.

The bottle breaks, the laughter dies,

The morning brings the hollow cries.

But giving, serving, standing still—

These joys the storms of time can't kill.

So seek not fire that scorches fast,

But light that's built to gently last.

For pleasure flees, and joy will stay—

When heart and truth don't turn away.

The Mirror of Mud and Gold

Aadhya sat near the monk Sahasrananda, eyes wide with wonder. The village was quiet that afternoon, wrapped in a slow golden light. Women stirred pots over open flames. A peaceful stillness hummed through the air.

Earlier that day, she had heard a man claim pleasure was found in wine and cards. Now, she sought something deeper.

"Joy…" she whispered aloud. "What is joy?"

The monk's eyes softened. A wind passed gently through the trees as if even nature paused to listen. He smiled and said:

"Let me narrate a story…"

"The young prince Devraj was beloved by the court, surrounded by music that sang his praises, feasts that celebrated his presence, and lovers who adorned his chambers like petals on a divine altar. From the outside, he had everything—fragrant oils, silk garments, rare fruits from distant lands.

But inside, something ached. A strange hollowness echoed in his laughter, a silence beneath the music.

One morning, restless and unfulfilled, he disguised himself as a wanderer and slipped out of the palace. He walked into a village wrapped in the scent of cow dung, cooked lentils, and dusty hope.

There, he saw an old woman struggling to carry water pots up a steep hill. Without a word, he took one pot and climbed beside her.

She didn't ask who he was. She just walked—slow, steady. At the top, breathless but smiling, she said, 'You've given more than water today. You've shared your strength.'

Something cracked open in him. Not with noise, but with light. Her joy was not gold-lined or perfumed—it was raw, honest, and strangely whole.

Devraj returned again and again. He helped, he listened, he learned. He ate with the villagers on the ground. He danced barefoot during festivals. He sang with children under mango trees.

One day, a courtier found him and said, 'The palace is mourning. Come back to your throne.'

But Devraj simply smiled. 'I've found a greater kingdom.'"

The monk looked at Aadhya.

"Pleasure," he said, "is often a song that fades after the echo. Joy is a silence that deepens the more you listen."

Then Aadhya, an inquisitive child, asked—

"What is a joy?" her voice unmasked.
Not wrapped in gold, nor soaked in wine,
But something that would always shine.

The monk replied with a gaze so kind,
"A joy is what the heart must find.
Not in the feast or praise or flame—
But in the act without a name.

Joy is the song that earthbirds sing
When hands reach out and hearts take wing.
It grows not loud, but grows so deep,
In quiet deeds that shadows keep.

It is the strength to lift another,
To feed the child, to serve the mother.
To laugh not from what one has gained,
But from the tears that love has trained.

It's walking barefoot through the rain,
And finding warmth inside your pain.
It's not escape, nor thrill, nor chase—
But resting soft in your own grace.

So if you seek what won't decay,

Give all your heart, then walk away.

For joy is found not when you try—

But when you give, and ask not why."

The Thirst That Consumes

The Orchard of Longing

One evening, as the golden dusk poured like honey over the village, a small gathering sat under the neem tree where Sahasrananda often rested. Birds rustled overhead, and the smoke from cooking fires curled like quiet prayers into the sky.

Vasudevan, a quiet seeker known for his thoughtful silence, finally spoke.

"When does pleasure cease to nourish, and begin to consume?" he asked, his voice steady, but heavy with experience.

The monk, brushing a fallen leaf from his robe, replied gently:

"When we seek it not for beauty, but for escape—when we devour instead of receive."

He paused, letting the wind carry the weight of his words.

Then he said, "Let me tell you a story..."

There was once a boy named Neel who lived beside a lush orchard. This orchard bore the juiciest mangoes—sweet, golden, kissed by sun and rain. Each season, the village celebrated the first ripe fruit. They plucked it with reverence, slicing it gently, sharing with neighbours, letting the nectar linger like a hymn upon their tongues.

Neel, as a child, had once savoured a mango so slowly that his eyes welled up with tears—not from sadness, but from the beauty of taste, of the sun distilled into sweetness.

But as he grew, something shifted. Life became harder—his father left, his mother fell ill. The world felt unpredictable, unforgiving.

One day, out of restlessness, he snuck into the orchard at night. He no longer ate the fruit with care. He devoured it. One, two, three mangoes at a time. He stuffed them into his bag. Juice dripped from his mouth. He wasn't tasting anymore—he was filling a hole.

The sweetness no longer comforted him. Yet he craved more.

Soon, the orchard lost its magic. It became only a place of escape—a place to forget his pain.

Years later, an old woman asked him, "Why do you eat as if you are starving when your belly is full?"

He didn't know.

She said gently, "You once loved the mango for its song. Now you only use it to silence your sorrow."

That night, Neel sat beneath the tree and did not eat. He listened. He remembered. And in the quiet, the taste of the mango returned—not on his tongue, but in his soul.

The monk turned to Vasudevan.

"Pleasure, when honoured, is like rain on parched earth. But when chased to numb pain, it becomes a flood that uproots the very roots it came to nourish."

He picked up a fallen fruit and held it gently.

"When we receive, we are grateful. When we devour, we are afraid. The difference lies not in the fruit, but in the hunger."

A mango ripened in the sun,

Soft gold beneath the sky's warm run.

One boy once tasted, slow and sweet,

He wept with joy—the world complete.

But pain came knocking, harsh and loud,

And joy withdrew beneath a cloud.

No longer did he taste or see,

He ate to drown, to cease, to flee.

He took not one, but took them all,

Still empty, though his belly full.

The fruit he loved, he now destroyed—

A silent prayer turned into a void.

Pleasure is not the flame we chase,

But warmth we feel in a still embrace.

When joy is used to dull the ache,

We find that sweetness starts to break.

So taste, but do not beg or bind,

Let fruit and soul remain aligned.

For when we seek not just to feel—

But to escape— we lose what's real.

Dances in the Rain

Monk after a pause said, "True joy is not the absence of pain, but the presence of awakened being. Escape avoids; joy accepts. One is numbness, the other is aliveness."

The Girl and the Storm

Monk said, "Let me narrate a story - They had gathered again near the lotus pond at twilight. A light drizzle had begun, and clouds rumbled in the distance. The villagers stayed under shelter, but Sahasrananda remained seated on the stone platform, his eyes lifted toward the sky."

Sam, always one to question what others dared not, leaned forward and asked, "What's the difference between escaping pain and embracing joy?"

The monk's eyes twinkled, and a soft smile crept onto his face.

"One runs away from the storm," he said, "the other dances in the rain. One numbs, the other awakens."

He paused, letting the breeze carry his silence, then said, "Let me tell you a story…"

There was once a girl named Kavya who feared thunder. As a child, every time it rumbled, she would hide beneath her bed, clutching her doll, covering her ears, waiting for it to pass. The storm, to her, was terror incarnate—an omen of all things unpredictable.

As she grew, life brought her storms of another kind: heartbreak, failure, death. And much like the thunder, she hid from them. She turned to distractions—noise, indulgence, even forced laughter. Parties with no depth, pleasures with no presence. She convinced herself she was living, but inside, she was merely waiting out the storm.

One day, in the middle of a festival, dark clouds gathered again. Everyone rushed inside. Kavya followed out of habit—but just as she reached the door, she saw an old man standing in the rain.

He was not afraid. In fact, he lifted his arms and laughed, letting the drops fall on his face. His joy was raw, alive. Something stirred in her.

She stepped back into the rain.

It was cold. It was wet. She trembled. But as she stood, something remarkable happened— She didn't run. She didn't hide. She let the storm pass through her.

She began to cry—not from fear, but from the strange relief of feeling everything at once.

That night, soaked and awake in a way she'd never known, she whispered to herself: "This… this is joy. Not an escape from pain. But a return to being real."

Sahasrananda looked up at the gentle rain now falling around them.

"Sam," he said softly, "To escape pain is to close your eyes and hope it goes away. To embrace joy is to open your arms and say, 'Even this is part of the dance.'"

He drew a circle in the wet earth with his finger.

"One path avoids feeling. The other deepens it. One shrinks your world. The other expands it until even pain becomes sacred."

I once ran from thunder's cry,

Fled each tear the sky let fall.

Built a roof of laughter high—

But dreams beneath it shrank so small.

I masked the ache in borrowed light,

Fed the hollow with delight.

But joy that's forged in numb disguise

Soon withers into silent lies.

Then came a storm I couldn't flee—

It soaked the mask, it entered me.

And in that downpour, fierce and true,

I met a self I never knew.

No longer running from the pain,

I danced beneath the tender rain.

And in that storm, I understood:

Joy doesn't bloom when all is good—

It rises when we cease to hide,

When even grief is seen inside.

It's not escape, nor gentle balm—

It's presence, raw. It's sacred calm.

And so, joy is not the absence of storms, but the courage to stand within them. It is not what shields us from life—but what lets life, in all its hues, touch us completely. To embrace joy is to say yes—even to the rain.

CHAPTER XIX

The Throne and the Puddle

"True wisdom does not arrive by summons, nor perform for applause—it walks barefoot, meeting only those who walk beside it."

– Shree Shambav

As the seasons passed, whispers of a monk named Sahasrananda echoed through every corner of the kingdom. His name was not uttered with fear like a ruler's, nor shouted with admiration like a hero's. It was spoken in soft reverence, in tea stalls and temple courtyards, in children's laughter and old women's prayers. He was a joy that wandered. The wisdom that did not preach.

Eventually, the king himself—who had long prided his name etched in stone and scroll—began to hear Sahasrananda's name more often than his own. On market streets, they spoke of the monk's teachings. In palace gardens, they sang his verses. This both intrigued and unsettled the king.

One evening, as twilight bathed the throne room in gold, he turned to his minister and said, "Find this monk. Invite him to my court—with honour."

The next morning, the minister, along with guards and offerings of fruit, incense, and silk, arrived at a humble village. Rain had just bathed the earth, and to their amazement, they found Sahasrananda in the muddy courtyard—laughing, barefoot, dancing in puddles with children, folding paper boats and racing them down a little stream.

His robes were wet, his beard dripping, but his face radiated an untamed joy that silenced even the most dutiful soldier.

When the rain paused, Sahasrananda bowed to the children, asking if he might speak with the guests. They nodded with the dignity of kings.

He welcomed the minister to his modest hut—no throne, no cushion, just the scent of wet earth and burning neem leaves.

The minister bowed and said, "Venerable one, by the King's command, we have come to escort you. He wishes to meet you, to understand your wisdom—for your name now rings louder than his."

Sahasrananda smiled gently. "Tell me then—why does your king wish to see me?"

"He is curious," the minister replied. "But he has sent us with honour, with offerings. Will you come?"

The monk gazed at the sky. The clouds above parted, spilling light through the banyan's branches. After a pause, he said softly, "If your king wishes to know me… then let him meet me not in command, but in communion. I am not a performer summoned by power. I meet only those who meet me as equals, not as owners."

The minister stiffened. "You do not understand, monk. Kings do not visit villagers. It is the people who go to the palace."

Sahasrananda gently closed his eyes. And then, in a quiet voice like falling rain, he recited a verse:

The mountain does not bend to man,

Though gold be thrown upon its feet.

A lamp does not chase royalty,

Its flame will burn for those who seek.

The sky does not to catch applause,

The river flows, yet asks no name.

Let those who thirst approach the spring,

Not cage it for the sake of fame.

Sahasrananda bowed once more—this time to the minister—and without another word, returned to the puddles, where the children waited with open arms and muddy feet.

Shocked and disoriented, the minister returned to the palace empty-handed.

The king listened in silence. His pride wrestled with his curiosity, like a lion pacing behind the bars of its own crown.

After a long pause, he said coldly, "Then ask the monk to leave my kingdom."

But that night, the king could not sleep.

He heard laughter in the rain. He saw a man who refused to bow—because he had already bowed… to truth.

Author's Note

This book was not written.

It was *received*—like a breeze that brushes past, whispering truths too gentle for loud minds. The silent monk, Sahasrananda, came to me not as a character but as a presence, as if he had always been there, sitting under the ancient banyan tree of my soul, waiting for me to listen.

Each story, each poem, emerged like petals from within a deep stillness. They reflect the questions that haunt us, the emotions that shape us, and the truths that liberate us—not just as individuals, but as a shared humanity. The tales are not merely about a village or a monk; they are fragments of your journey and mine, echoes of universal longings and awakenings.

The structure of this book—woven with poetry, story, and reflection—was chosen to mirror life's own rhythm: the rising and falling of hope, the blooming of love, the ache of letting go, and the silent wisdom that follows.

I offer this work not as a teacher, but as a fellow traveller. May these pages hold space for your own questions, tears, revelations, and returns. If somewhere between the silences, you meet a part of yourself you had forgotten… then the monk has done his work.

In silence,

Shree Shambav

Life Coach and Philanthropist

Shree Shambav is the visionary founder of the Shree Shambav Ayur Rakshita Foundation (www.shambav-ayurrakshita.org). He founded this institution with a lofty goal: to recognise human identity across gender, ethnicity, and nationality. Through this organisation, he wants to assist all communities in realising their full potential and the intrinsic beauty of life.

Shree Shambav, a Life Coach, is dedicated to supporting people on their journeys of self-discovery and empowerment. He assists people in discovering who they are, determining what inspires and drives them, and overcoming limiting ideas. His approach clarifies what one wants in life, assisting people through goal-setting and a step-by-step process for achieving them. He empowers people to make deliberate and responsible decisions, allowing them to identify their blind spots and evolve as individuals via the use of numerous strategies and tools.

The foundation's bold, uncompromising, and compassionate ventures are always aimed at initiating the "Inner Transformation" process. They focus on spiritual growth, personal growth, and self-healing while emphasising that true progress lies in "Inclusive Growth and Co-existence." This philosophy drives all their initiatives, encouraging a holistic approach to development and well-being.

Under Shree Shambav's leadership, the foundation has launched several impactful movements:

Shree Shambav Green Movement: This mission is to create a healthy, green, and clean earth through responsible water conservation and greening initiatives. The movement strives to make the world a green paradise by encouraging sustainable living and environmental responsibility.

Shree Shambav Vidya Vedhika (Vizhuthugal): This project aims to help students and children by offering training, books, stationery, and uniforms. It aims to provide the next generation with the tools and resources they need to excel both academically and personally.

Shree Shambav and his foundation exemplify the spirit of compassion, transformation, and inclusive growth via their work, which has a profound impact on individuals and communities around the world. His work exemplifies the power of acknowledging and nourishing the human spirit, creating a world in which everyone can reach their full potential and appreciate the beauty of life.

ACKNOWLEDGEMENTS

To my grandfathers, grandmothers, mothers, fathers, aunts, uncles, neighbours, sisters, brothers, friends, and teachers, they poured in endless moral stories, retellings of Ramayana, Mahabharata, Puranas, Upanishads, and so on.

My teachers, neighbours, and kindred souls. Who provided us with a stage to perform wonderful Puranic stories and were gracious enough to acknowledge our efforts.

The artists and translators of epics have served as a source of inspiration, invigorating our spirits, making these works accessible, and enabling us to grasp the profound depths and deeper dimensions they contain.

I also cherish the stimulating conversations; I had with my wonderful mothers, Punitha Muniswamy and Uma Devi.

Our family's youngest member, Aadhya, who always overwhelmed me with questions, inspired this book.

I would likewise prefer to express gratitude to Mr Sivakumar, Mrs Roopa Sivakumar, Mr Akshaya Rajesh, Ms Akshatha Rajesh, Ms Apeksha Prabhu, Mr

Akanksh Prabhu, Mr Nikash Sarasambi, and Mrs Spoorthi Nikash for their valuable inputs.

I must thank Mr Rajesh, Mr Savan Prabhu, Mrs Revathi Rajesh, Mrs Rajani Sarasambi, and Mrs Manju Reshma, who encouraged me and often suggested writing a book. Their unwavering belief that I had something valuable to offer kept me going during my writing sessions.

Love you all,

Shree Shambav

www.shambav.org

shreeshambav@gmail.com

9 789356 194250

Printed at Repro India Ltd.